✗ PROTECTED MODE

A mode of 80286 and later processors in which they can address 16MB (for a 286) or 4GB (for a 386 and later) of memory, and in which the operating system can control memory use by applications.

✗ RAM

Random access memory. Memory that can be written to as well as read from, and whose contents are volatile, disappearing when power is lost.

✗ RAM DISK

A simulation of a disk drive created in RAM, used because of its great speed.

✗ REAL MODE

A processor mode in which the processor emulates the PC's original 8088 chip, allowing it access to only 1MB of memory.

✗ ROM

Read-only memory. Memory whose contents are permanent, used to store instructions for operating hardware.

✗ ROM BIOS

One or more blocks of ROM loaded high in upper memory, which hold instructions used to perform basic functions in your PC, including starting it and loading the operating system.

✗ ROM SHADOWING

A technique used in many PCs to speed processing by substituting RAM for ROM in upper memory, but making the original instructions available at their old addresses.

STANDARD MODE

A Windows operating mode that uses only features available on an 80286 processor. It can run only one DOS application at a time and has certain other restrictions.

TSR

Terminate-and-stay-resident program; also called simply a resident program. A TSR is a program loaded into DOS memory from the DOS command prompt or a batch file that remains loaded and active after you exit it. Resident programs receive control through interrupts, such as result from keyboard activity, and perform various functions. Pop-ups are resident programs that appear on the screen and allow you to work with them after you press a special hot key.

✗ UPPER MEMORY

Also called the upper memory area. The address range from 640K to 1MB, used to hold BIOS instructions, video memory, and (using a memory manager) software device-drivers and resident programs.

✗ V86 MODE

Also called virtual 8086 mode. A mode of 80386 and later processors, which emulates real mode but retains the controls over memory available under 386 enhanced mode.

✗ VCPI

Virtual Control Program Interface. A standard for programs to obtain extended memory from a memory manager and then to operate from that memory, in protected mode.

✗ VDS

Virtual DMA Services. A standard for intermediating between a hardware device (like an SCSI controller) that uses direct memory access and maintains a buffer at a fixed memory location on the one hand, and a protected-mode operating environment that may remap memory on the other hand. VDS is implemented as a device driver for the hardware device.

✗ VIRTUAL MEMORY

A disk file holding a direct image of memory contents, used to create a simulation of more physical memory than is actually available.

✗ XBDA

Extended BIOS data area. A 1K or larger area created by some PCs at the top of conventional memory to record system data.

✗ XMS

Extended Memory Specification. An evolving standard for how memory managers allocate upper memory, the High Memory Area, or extended memory to other programs.

Computer users are not all alike.
Neither are SYBEX books.

We know our customers have a variety of needs. They've told us so. And because we've listened, we've developed several distinct types of books to meet the needs of each of our customers. What are you looking for in computer help?

If you're looking for the basics, try the **ABC's** series. You'll find short, unintimidating tutorials and helpful illustrations. For a more visual approach, select **Teach Yourself,** featuring screen-by-screen illustrations of how to use your latest software purchase.

Running Start books are really two books in one—a tutorial to get you off to a fast start and a reference to answer your questions when you're ready to tackle advanced tasks.

Mastering and **Understanding** titles offer you a step-by-step introduction, plus an in-depth examination of intermediate-level features, to use as you progress.

Our **Up & Running** series is designed for computer-literate consumers who want a no-nonsense overview of new programs. Just 20 basic lessons, and you're on your way.

We also publish two types of reference books. Our **Instant References** provide quick access to each of a program's commands and functions. SYBEX **Encyclopedias** and **Desktop References** provide a *comprehensive reference* and explanation of all of the commands, features, and functions of the subject software.

Our **Programming** books are specifically written for a technically sophisticated audience and provide a no-nonsense value-added approach to each topic covered, with plenty of tips, tricks, and time-saving hints.

Sometimes a subject requires a special treatment that our standard series don't provide. So you'll find we have titles like **Advanced Techniques, Handbooks, Tips & Tricks,** and others that are specifically tailored to satisfy a unique need.

We carefully select our authors for their in-depth understanding of the software they're writing about, as well as their ability to write clearly and communicate effectively. Each manuscript is thoroughly reviewed by our technical staff to ensure its complete accuracy. Our production department makes sure it's easy to use. All of this adds up to the highest quality books available, consistently appearing on best-seller charts worldwide.

You'll find SYBEX publishes a variety of books on every popular software package. Looking for computer help? Help Yourself to SYBEX.

 ### For a brochure of our best-selling publications:

SYBEX Inc., 2021 Challenger Drive, Alameda, CA 94501
SYBEX Tel: (510) 523-8233/(800) 227-2346 Telex: 336311
Fax: (510) 523-2373

SYBEX is committed to using natural resources wisely to preserve and improve our environment. As a leader in the computer book publishing industry, we are aware that over 40% of America's solid waste is paper. This is why we have been printing the text of books like this one on recycled paper since 1982.

This year our use of recycled paper will result in the saving of more than 15,300 trees. We will lower air pollution effluents by 54,000 pounds, save 6,300,000 gallons of water, and reduce landfill by 2,700 cubic yards.

In choosing a SYBEX book you are not only making a choice for the best in skills and information, you are also choosing to enhance the quality of life for all of us.

BEYOND

THE LIMITS:

SECRETS OF

PC MEMORY

MANAGEMENT

BEYOND

THE LIMITS:

SECRETS OF

PC MEMORY

MANAGEMENT

Bob Campbell

SYBEX ®

San Francisco
Paris
Düsseldorf
Soest

Acquisitions Editor: David J. Clark
Developmental Editor: Gary Masters
Editor: Richard Mills
Technical Editor: Barry Schnur
Book Designer: Ingrid Owen
Technical Illustrations and Screen Graphics : Cuong Le
Desktop Publishing Specialist: Thomas Goudie
Production Assistant: Lisa Haden
Indexer: Ted Laux
Cover Designer: Archer Design
Cover Photographer: Mark Johann
Photo Art Direction: Ingalls + Associates

Screen reproductions produced with Collage Plus.

Collage Plus is a trademark of Inner Media Inc.

SYBEX is a registered trademark of SYBEX Inc.

Library of Congress Card Number: 92-82840

ISBN: 0-7821-1161-0

Manufactured in the United States of America

10 9 8 7 6 5 4 3 2 1

ACKNOWLEDGMENTS

I am happy to thank Gary Masters for the initial concept of this book and much creative interaction in shaping up its organization and presentation, Richard Mills for careful editing, Barry Schnur, technical reviewer, for bringing up many useful points, and Cuong Le for taking time to make inventive renderings of the many figures. Thanks to JoAnn and Sunshine (the one with the sunspots) for not allowing me to become too fixated on untangling all these knots.

CONTENTS AT A GLANCE

TABLE OF CONTENTS

✗ APPENDICES

INTRODUCTION

So you have a 386 or 486 PC with 4, 8, 16 or more megabytes of RAM. What can DOS do with all that memory? What does it take to make best use of all of it? As it turns out, it takes a product called a *memory manager,* plus a little understanding on your part, to know what you are asking of the memory manager and how to solve the problems that sometimes arise.

DOS 5 comes with means for memory management, but there are commercial packages that go far beyond it in ability to make the most of your PC's memory. They are also easier to use. Two of the best, as well as the most popular, of these packages are QEMM from Quarterdeck and 386MAX from Qualitas.

Beyond the Limits: Secrets of PC Memory Management is the book you need to learn painlessly how to make the most of your memory, whether you're using only DOS and Windows or have purchased QEMM or 386MAX. It offers you the perspective on PC memory concepts you need to make sense of the sometimes jargon-ridden documentation for these products and to select from their numerous options knowledgeably. It also reconciles the sometimes conflicting terminology used by DOS and Windows on the one hand and by Quarterdeck and Qualitas on the other.

This book covers DOS through version 5, Windows through version 3.1, QEMM through version 6.03, and 386MAX through version 6.02.

WHO THIS BOOK IS FOR

Beyond the Limits assumes no prior understanding of memory management techniques and concepts. You also don't need any special knowledge of DOS, although a basic knowledge of how to enter DOS commands, navigate the drive and directory structure, and work with files is helpful. Even if you are familiar with memory management, you will find this book full of useful information on how to use QEMM and 386MAX.

Learning how to manage memory on your PC can be different from learning other kinds of computer skills. When you learned word processing, for example, you probably learned it progressively, beginning with simple tasks and moving on to more complex operations. Using a memory manager tends to be very simple (run the programs to install the manager and optimize the setup) until you need to do something special. Then, you may find yourself in a thicket of obscure concepts. *Beyond the Limits* uses a step-by-step approach to help you understand computer memory by introducing the basic concepts and how they are put to work in your PC before it covers the advanced features of a memory management package.

Accordingly, the book is designed to give everyone the proper background and then clarify the more arcane features. However, if you are already familiar with memory terms and how PC memory is organized, you can skim the first part for unfamiliar concepts and then learn to work with your chosen memory manager. If you just need to know how to solve a particular problem, the index will guide you to the right section.

One feature of this book that will aid your understanding is the sidebars, especially in the early chapters. These sidebars explain basic memory concepts; they are designed to make these concepts tangible through analogies from ordinary experience. Reading one of them may provoke the "Aha!" response, in which a concept that was opaque suddenly becomes transparent, a realization that you can apply directly to your work.

HOW THIS BOOK IS ORGANIZED

Beyond the Limits is in three parts. Part I introduces PC memory concepts and how they apply to the popular operating environments DOS and Windows:

Chapter 1 provides you with an overview of what memory is, what kinds of memory there are, how your PC's central processing unit addresses memory, and what goes on within the notorious 640K and 1MB limits on DOS memory.

Chapter 2 describes what lies beyond the 1MB DOS limit. It clarifies the difference between *expanded memory* and *extended memory,* as well as shows how memory managers provide services to programs that call upon the advanced features of 386 and later processors for memory use.

Chapter 3 covers how DOS manages memory and how to use DOS 5 features in conjunction with your memory manager.

Chapter 4 answers your questions about Windows versions 3.0 and 3.1: how to choose an operating mode, how to get Windows to cooperate with QEMM or 386MAX, how to make best use of extended memory, how to use Windows SMARTDrive, how to optimize Windows' own use of memory, and more.

Parts II and III of this book are parallel treatments of the memory manager products themselves, with Part II (Chapters 5 through 7) devoted to QEMM and Part III (Chapters 8 through 10) devoted to 386MAX. You can study the chapters that apply to your memory manager, or read through all six chapters as an aid to evaluating the two products.

The chapters are arranged in this way:

Chapter 5 (on QEMM) and **Chapter 8** (on 386MAX) guide you through installing the products and optimizing them for your system. These chapters then introduce the supplemental programs and reporting services each package offers.

Chapters 6 and 9 offer a tour of the advanced programs in each package for learning about your system and studying in detail how it uses memory. The chapters then show you how to analyze your PC's memory use and how to identify problem areas and opportunities. Finally, they provide tips and techniques for resolving problems with common hardware and software combinations.

Chapters 7 and 10 are command references that show you how to use the many options to the memory managers themselves and to the utilities that come with them.

Finally, this book includes two appendices: The first is a simple introduction to the hexadecimal numbering that you will encounter so frequently in working with memory addresses (the strange numbers that include letters A through F). The second is a guide to buying and installing memory on your PC.

Now you can get started with Chapter 1 and begin to learn how your PC uses memory.

✗ PART I

ONE ⟫

Part I provides the background information you need to make the most of your memory manager. Chapter 1 covers the basic types and uses of memory in your PC as well as the specifics of how DOS uses the first megabyte of memory. Chapter 2 describes memory beyond the 1MB limit and explains the difference between extended and expanded memory (and the respective XMS and EMS standards for using them). It also introduces the idea of protected-mode operation. Chapters 3 and 4 include specific information on memory management with DOS 5 and Windows, an environment that makes great demands on your system's memory.

CHAPTER ONE

THE

LIMITS

OF

MEMORY

It's obvious to anyone who works much with PCs these days that shortage of memory is becoming a crisis, but you must understand the dimensions of PC memory to deal with the problem effectively. Memory shortfalls are a product of the PC's design and evolution. *Memory managers* like Quarterdeck's QEMM and Qualitas's 386MAX, plus your 386 or 486 PC, come to your rescue, offering you efficient use of every byte of memory in your system. Although they take over much of the work of memory management for you, a little knowledge will go a long way in helping you make best use of one of these tools.

WHY ADDRESS MEMORY?

It would seem reasonable to buy and install enough memory to run your applications and then to get on with your work. However, the PC has evolved in ways that require you to take a more active approach and to learn how to make the best use of available memory. Fortunately, the basic concepts are simple to grasp.

The original IBM PC came to the market complete with a bare *16K* of RAM installed, not even enough to load recent versions of DOS. You could upgrade your PC to 64K. The 640K of RAM possible under the PC's essential design seemed like the wild blue yonder in the early days of personal computing.

The shortcomings of even the 640K limit first became painfully apparent as people began devising huge spreadsheets using Lotus 1-2-3 or other programs. Also, as time went on, many applications grew more complex and made more demands on memory. For example, word processors began to offer WYSIWYG ("What You See Is What You Get") graphics displays, and all kinds of programs with easy-to-use interface designs were introduced that demanded great behind-the-scenes programming complexity. Maybe the coup de grace was the advent and development of Microsoft Windows, with all its power and sophistication.

As applications evolved, PC users came to rely on an ever-growing variety of systems tools, ranging from disk caches to pop-up appointment books, each of which made its own demands on DOS memory. DOS itself has grown more complex as it has risen to such fresh demands as networking.

By now, 640K is a very cramped space. To move beyond this limit, you must know what kind of additional memory you need and how to use it.

UNDERSTANDING MEMORY

At the heart of your PC is the integrated circuit chip known as the *central processing unit,* or *CPU* for short, which is responsible for loading and running your applications, accepting your keystrokes, handling all your data, making calculations, creating your screens, and undertaking all the other actions that lie at the heart of computing.

When you start an application and open a file (say, a document or a spreadsheet), the program and the file are read from disk storage into memory, which is composed of integrated circuits, where the CPU can manipulate them quickly. When you have finished working with the file, you write it back to disk storage.

Memory is thus a kind of scratch pad for the CPU. The numerical values in your spreadsheet, the words in your word-processed document, the screens that you see displayed, and the instructions that the CPU must consult at each step it takes are found in memory. Beyond this, the operating system (DOS) and the low-level instructions (the BIOS, or Basic Input/Output System) that intermediate between your applications and the computer hardware reside in memory. As all these systems become more complex and sophisticated, their demands for memory increase. The first limit on the amount of memory you can use is fixed by the design of the CPU itself.

THE CENTRAL PROCESSING UNIT

The CPU is the chip in your PC that undertakes all of what we usually think of as computing, operating on data in memory. The CPU recognizes a primitive set of operations known as *instructions*. All of the high-level design of an application must be devolved into a long set of instructions, and all of your input to the program (for instance, all that you type) must be interpreted according to these instructions, which are also held in memory.

If you were to compare a PC with a car, the CPU would be the engine, which carries out a small number of repetitive operations at high speed. The engine takes in a mix of fuel and air, processes them by compressing and igniting them, and produces output in the form of mechanical energy. The CPU receives a series of simple instructions and raw data and processes them: For instance, it may add two numbers when it receives an ADD instruction, or it may copy a value to a new location in memory when it receives a MOV instruction. Your PC does everything in terms of simple steps like these. In this way, the CPU consumes raw data and produces work in the form of processed information. In other words, both the engine and the PC do their work through a small number of simple operations, no matter where you are driving or what your PC application is.

Addressing Memory

The CPU has two channels for addressing memory (referring to memory, designating a point from which to read or to which to write): the *data bus* and the *address bus*. The data bus is the channel through which your data actually pass to and from the CPU. Accordingly, the wider and faster the bus, the faster your CPU can process data. The value placed on the address bus names the exact point in memory to which an item of data will be written or from which it will be retrieved. The wider this bus, the larger the number it can represent, and so the greater the amount of memory the CPU can address. Although the width of the data bus and the speed of memory access are of keen interest to you as a computer buyer,

DOS AND THE BIOS

DOS and the BIOS are closely related systems in your PC. One of the main differences between them is that the first resides on disk and the second is programmed onto chips on your PC's motherboard. Also, DOS functions tend to be higher-level and more general than BIOS functions; BIOS functions generally deal with handling devices, such as disk drives and video. DOS functions additionally deal with tasks of allocating memory to programs and preparing them to run.

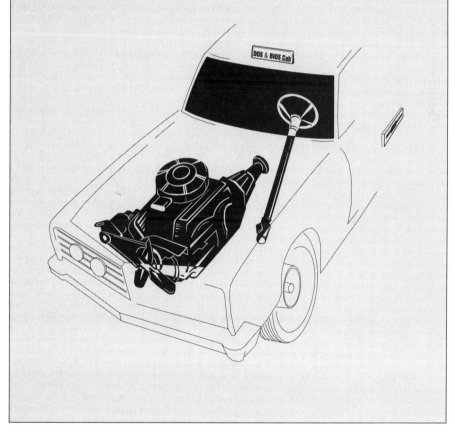

> To continue the automobile analogy, DOS generally corresponds to the higher-level systems of the car that you use more or less directly, but the BIOS is more like the lower-level, deeper systems that control the engine and car. For instance, DOS (in the form of the command processor that handles the DOS prompt) is like the steering wheel; the BIOS is more like the steering linkage. For another example, DOS is like the accelerator linkage; the BIOS is like the carburetor or fuel injectors. Finally, DOS is like the electrical switches, and the BIOS is like the alternator, relays, distributor, and so forth.

the limitations of the address bus are what make PC memory management such a pressing issue.

These buses are sets of lines (in part, conductive traces on your computer's motherboard). Through the rules of binary arithmetic, the CPU can turn each address line on or off to form an address in memory. Suppose there were only one address line: It could be either on or off, representing memory locations with the "street addresses" 0 or 1. If there were two address lines, four permutations would be possible: 00, 01, 10, and 11 (0, 1, 2, and 3). The amount of space that the CPU can address turns out to be 2 raised to the power of the number of lines. The CPU addresses memory as *bytes*, which are sets of eight simple on/off states (*bits*), so this power of 2 is the number of bytes that your CPU can potentially use. This number is conventionally given in *kilobytes* (KB, or just K), *megabytes* (MB), or even *gigabytes* (GB). A kilobyte is not exactly a thousand bytes but rather 2^{10}, or 1024, bytes. A megabyte is 2^{10} kilobytes, or 1,048,576 bytes. A gigabyte is 2^{10} megabytes, or 1,073,741,824 bytes—much more memory than this is not of practical value at present.

As the PC has evolved and new generations of CPUs have arrived, bus widths have kept increasing. Here are the widths of the data and address buses of the various generations of Intel CPUs that have been used in PCs. Remember that the address bus width is critical to how much memory can be used.

THE DATA BUS AND THE ADDRESS BUS

The CPU always must approach memory in terms first of Where? and then of What?: Where in memory am I to read or write, then what is there? (Or, what is to be written there?) Each of these questions relates to bandwidth and speed: How much memory can I address? How fast can I identify a location? How fast can I read or write to a location, and how big a chunk can I read or write at a time?

When you go to a library, you encounter a similar situation: If you want a particular title, you must go to the catalog and get a reference number (the address) and then use the number to go to the shelves to retrieve the book it-self (the data). The number has two parts: The part before the period gives you the main subject, and the part after the period gives you a subclassification (plus the author's initials). This is curiously like PC memory addresses, which always have a major part (the segment or the selector) and a minor part (the offset), as you will learn in the next chapter.

CHAPTER ONE

> If you obtain books from a library's stacks, you are concerned with how many books you can retrieve at one time: Can you check out one, two, or four books with a single request? This becomes the limiting factor in how fast you can obtain information. The width of the data bus is important in just this way, because it determines how many data items the CPU can refer to in a single time interval.

PROCESSOR	DATA BUS WIDTH (IN BITS)	ADDRESS BUS WIDTH (IN BITS)	ADDRESS SPACE
8088	8	20	1MB
8086	16	20	1MB
80286	16	24	16MB
80386SX	16	24	16MB
80386	32	32	4GB
i486, i486SX	32	32	4GB

The 80386 is also known as a 386DX, or just a 386. Its little sister, the 80386SX, is configured *internally* like an 80386, so it can manipulate 32-bit data as well as all the 80386 instructions. Externally, however, it treats memory as an 80286 does. The i486SX is a stripped-down version of the i486 that addresses memory as its larger cousin does. (The i486 was itself previously known as the 80486.)

Note the 1MB limit on memory for the 8088 CPU, the chip around which the PC and DOS were originally designed. Because DOS and today's applications are so bound to the limits of this chip, later processors must emulate it when they are running DOS. Thus, they are themselves limited to 1MB of memory. The mode in which these processors emulate an 8088 is known as *real mode,* but their native mode is known as *protected mode,* for reasons that will be explained in the next chapter. You already know that, of this 1MB of memory, 640K traditionally has been available for DOS and your applications. It's time to see what kinds of memory go to make up the entire megabyte.

BITS AND BYTES

A byte is a small area of memory or storage subdivided into eight smaller areas called bits. The bits are like slots that can be occupied or not. The number and pattern of occupied bits determine the value held by the byte. Bytes are, in effect, lined up end to end to compose larger units of memory.

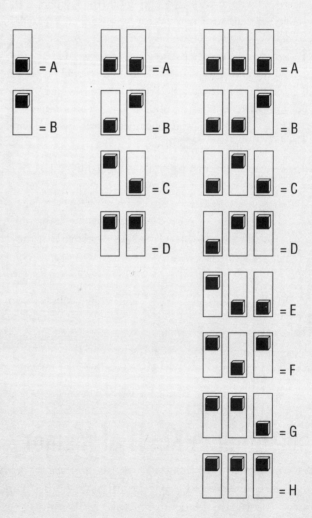

A byte is something like a set of eight switches, each of which can have either of two values, *on* or *off*. (This particular analogy can take on almost literal significance; one of the first microcomputers had as its only input device a bank of eight switches, which you could use to load data one byte at a time.) The value of the byte is any permutation of the setting for all the switches.

It's easy to visualize the possibilities offered by one or two switches. For instance, a single switch can be either on or off (the left part of the illustration). If the values that we wanted to represent were uppercase letters of the alphabet, that one switch would suffice to represent A and B. If we had two switches (the middle part of the illustration), they would have four permutations—both off could represent A; #1 on and #2 off could represent B; #1 off and #2 on could represent C; and both on could represent D. You can see how the possibilities reflect powers of 2—the four permutations, for instance, are the number 2 to the power of the number of switches (2). Three switches give 2 to the 3rd, or 8, total possibilities.

Sometimes in computing, you will see an eighth switch, or rather an eighth bit, used as a check on the value of the other seven. For instance, if an odd number of bits are on, the eighth bit will also be turned on to make the total number turned on even. When you check the settings and see that the total number is even, this offers some assurance that the settings are correct. This concept is called *even parity*, which you may encounter in telecommunications.

Your PC also uses parity to check values in its memory. In this case, the eight bits are used for data and a ninth is used as a parity bit to check the others. This is why, when adding memory, you insert nine DRAM chips in a bank, or why there are nine chips on a SIMM or a SIP assembly. (You will read more about these forms of RAM in Appendix B.)

Understanding Kinds of Memory

Memory comes in two basic forms, *random access memory* (RAM) and *read-only memory* (ROM). Actually, the name "random access memory" is a bit misleading, because both kinds of memory are random access; that is, the CPU can call up any arbitrary address directly without reading sequentially through lower addresses. RAM is really read-write memory, which the processor can use as a scratch pad and modify rapidly. ROM is memory that contains preset instructions and data, often for controlling physical devices like disk drives associated with the PC.

RAM AND ROM

RAM and ROM are the two basic types of memory that you will find in your PC. Both are semiconductor memory found on chips. Forget about the full name of the first kind—random access memory—all the memory in your PC is random access. RAM is read-write memory; ROM, as the full name says, is read-only memory.

ROM is used to hold instructions to control devices, which never change. This is what the BIOS of your PC largely consists of: instructions for controlling hardware. The hardware is built into the PC, so the BIOS instructions specific to that hardware are likewise built into it, as ROM. If you install a custom video adapter, it includes its own BIOS instructions on ROM, which will replace the built-in instructions every time you boot up the machine. RAM is used for data that come and go. RAM is typically a good deal faster than ROM.

As an analogy, if you walk into a classroom, you will likely see blackboards as well as printed charts. The charts (depending on the level) may show letters of the alphabet, formulas, maps, and so forth. They may be continually referred to during classes, but their contents never change. If they become out-of-date (and funding allows), they are replaced. The blackboards, on the other hand, are erased and written over again and again, with important points from the lecture, exercises, illustrations, and assignments. Plainly, the contents of the charts and the blackboards differ in kind—the charts show basic facts that must be on hand in a variety of contexts, and the blackboards show information of significance at the moment. ROM is like the charts, and RAM is like the blackboards.

RAM

RAM is the essential memory and occupies up to the first 640K of your PC's address space, as well as anywhere else that the contents of memory may change, such as the video buffer or expanded or extended memory (described in Chapter 2). The RAM that makes up the bulk of your PC's memory is called *dynamic RAM,* or *DRAM,* because it must be frequently recharged, or *refreshed,* to preserve its contents. The recharging steps slow it down somewhat.

RAM chips are organized in banks of nine: When the CPU stores a byte of data, 1 bit from the byte goes into a pigeonhole in each chip of a bank. The ninth chip holds a special parity bit that acts as a check on the correctness of the values in the other eight. When your computer accepts memory in the form of *SIPs* (*single in-line packages*) or *SIMMs* (*single in-line memory modules*), all the chips in a bank are combined on a single card that you can insert. When you buy chips of a given size rating, the rating gives the number of bytes that a whole bank of these chips will hold. For instance, a bank of 256K chips will hold 256K bytes of data.

TIP

If you are adding RAM to your PC, there are several things you should note for compatibility and greatest speed. For instance, you should always fill the motherboard or proprietary expansion card of your 80386 or i486 PC before adding memory to an add-on card. This is because the CPU uses a 32-bit data path in addressing motherboard memory, which is much faster than the 16-bit path on the standard PC bus. Also, you must buy chips that can be read and written fast enough for your computer. You can read more about how to buy and install RAM in Appendix B.

Besides this garden variety of RAM, you will encounter some specialized forms of RAM as you deal with memory management.

Video RAM The video buffer is a specialized area of memory where the CPU composes in detail the image that appears on your screen. Memory here is specially organized to handle such qualities of the presentation as color, but it occupies part of the address space like other memory. The video buffer starts at 640K, but its size and memory locations depend on the video mode in use.

For instance, a video mode may be either a *text mode* or a *graphics mode.* In text mode, the CPU uses a couple of bytes of video buffer space to prescribe what character will appear at any position on your screen and what color it will appear in. The video adapter takes over the task of forming the characters. DOS-based word processors and spreadsheets usually use text mode, which is very fast and demands a relatively small amount of buffer space. As you will learn, if you use text mode exclusively, your memory manager may be able to reclaim some address space assigned to the video buffer for conventional memory.

TEXT MODE VS. GRAPHICS MODE

Your video display is always a form of dot matrix, a two-dimensional grid of points, where each dot must be painted a particular color so that the whole screen forms a pattern of text characters, graphics designs, or both. The difference between text mode and graphics mode lies in what subsystem of your PC is responsible for painting each dot, or pixel.

In text mode, the CPU treats the screen as a grid of characters (usually 80×25) and uses two bytes of video memory to name each character and its attribute or color. The graphics adapter forms and displays the character, resulting in very fast display and efficient use of address space. Early video adapters could use only a font contained in their ROM, but more recent (EGA and later) adapters can accept any font created in computer memory. Applications can, in fact, simulate graphics displays by creating parts of an image character-cell-by-character-cell and downloading that image to the card like a font—a process called *tiling*. The current Norton Utilities and PC Tools shell programs use this process, which creates a graphics screen that can be changed very quickly. In graphics mode itself, the CPU dictates directly how each pixel will appear. This makes it easy for software to create a graphics image on-screen, but it requires more RAM to contain values for each pixel and more CPU time to manipulate each pixel.

You can imagine a video display as being like the cards held up at a football game to display messages, where each participant seated in the bleachers is a pixel, and you, the CPU, are directing the stunts. In graphics mode, you would have to tell each participant in detail exactly which card to hold up. This takes some time, but it is very flexible. In text mode, you could just shout, "Give me an F," and everyone would know what color card to hold up to help form the character. As far as you are concerned, in fact, a few participants could just unfurl big canvas banners, each displaying a fully formed letter, like in the illustration.

All Windows-based programs, as well as presentation graphics and CAD programs, use a graphics mode to display images. In this case, the CPU must specify the color value for each *pixel*, or dot, on-screen, and demands on video buffer space are greater.

Cache Memory   Using a cache is a means of speeding access to data by moving them to a fast medium if they are likely to be read or modified soon. For instance, if data have just been read, they are likely to be read again soon, and so are the data that follow them.

The inexpensive DRAM chips used for main memory are not able to keep up with fast 80386 or i486 processors. For this reason, manufacturers often design PCs to include small amounts of expensive *SRAM* (*static RAM,* which does not have to be refreshed frequently) as a *hardware cache.* The presence of a hardware cache should be transparent to your memory manager and not influence its handling of main memory.

Another technique for speeding access to memory is *interleaving,* in which sequential data items are assigned to alternate banks of memory, allowing one bank to be refreshed as the next is being read or modified. Like the hardware cache, this mechanism is handled by low-level hardware and is not something you need to worry about.

Another form of cache memory is a *software cache,* which is a block of memory assigned to hold data from disk drives. Depending on how often your applications have to access data from disk, an effective cache can speed your work greatly, since memory accesses are much faster than disk accesses. A software cache can be created in extended memory (described in Chapter 2) and justifies having plenty of memory in your computer.

Some disk controllers include caches built onto the card. When these caches are reasonably large (a half-megabyte to several megabytes), they are functionally equivalent to a software cache created in main memory. Software caches are generally just as fast, however, and considerably cheaper.

CACHE MEMORY

A cache is somewhere to place frequently used items to make them more readily available than they would be otherwise. A software cache is located in RAM to hold frequently used items read from disk, because RAM access is always faster than disk access. A hardware cache is located in faster-than-usual RAM. You obtain the means to create a software cache from a third-party software maker, but a hardware cache is either built into your PC or not.

Picture a well-organized desk. A collection of frequently used items arranged on the desktop is like a hardware cache. The desk drawers are like RAM: If one drawer has been carefully set aside for materials needed for a current project, it is like a software cache. In terms of computer time, information stored on disk is like stuff in boxes piled in the closet, attic, or garage. You may even have to go through several boxes to find what you need. In short, it may take hundreds of times as long to find items in the boxes as items right at your desk.

For now, note the essential difference between the two kinds of cache: The software cache (or the caching disk controller) speeds access to data on the disk by keeping recently used disk data in memory, but the hardware cache (or the on-board cache) speeds access to memory itself by keeping recently used data in yet faster memory. The two classes of cache, in serving different functions, are compatible, and each will speed up your computer. On the other hand, there is generally nothing to be gained by employing two kinds of software cache, or both a software cache and a caching controller, because one only duplicates the efforts of the other, and there is extra overhead.(The software cache will generally prove to be as fast as or faster than the caching controller, as well as quite a bit cheaper.) Some PCs, however, make profitable use of the i486's on-board cache and of an additional hardware cache.

Note that a caching controller on a disk drive is no different in principle from a software cache in main memory—the cache is simply on the controller card instead of in main memory. Likewise, the cache incorporated into an i486 CPU serves the same function as a hardware cache: It speeds access to data and instructions in main memory.

ROM

As mentioned, memory whose contents cannot ordinarily be modified is read-only memory, or ROM, which usually contains instructions for operating physical devices, including the PC itself.

When you first turn on, reset, or reboot your PC, it is under the control of code in ROM (known as the ROM BIOS) located near the upper end of the basic 1MB address space. Then, additional devices in your computer take over blocks of unused address space to insert the ROM code containing instructions for their specialized uses. For instance, your video adapter will locate its own block of ROM in the area of memory just above that assigned to the video buffer. Hard-disk drives, network adapter cards, and other devices will take over areas between the video ROM area and the ROM BIOS area. Normally, this process will leave open spaces in the memory map—a condition that memory managers exploit heavily.

Not all the memory in your computer occupies this first megabyte. As you will read in the next chapter, *extended* memory lies beyond this limit, and *expanded* memory exists outside the normal PC address space and is read into the first megabyte on demand, in blocks. Other memory, such as the CMOS RAM that holds the PC's setup information, is read through an entirely different CPU subsystem, called the *Port I/O system*, which also communicates with devices like serial and parallel I/O cards.   Now you're in a position to understand how these forms of RAM and ROM are placed within the basic first megabyte of address space.

Understanding Areas of Memory

Figure 1.1 shows the general contents of the first megabyte of memory from the ground up. This section takes a quick look at what these contents are.

Conventional Memory

Also known as *base memory*, conventional memory is the classic 640K of address space allocated to RAM for DOS and your applications. If you don't actually have the full 640K installed in your PC, no upgrade is simpler or more worthwhile. We'll take a close look at how programs fit into this area of RAM in the section "Focus on Conventional Memory."

The Upper Memory Area

The *upper memory area* (UMA) is the part of the memory map extending from the top of conventional memory up to the 1MB DOS limit—384K all told. Just to make matters confusing, it is sometimes called *reserved memory* because it is normally reserved for BIOS for devices like video cards, disk controllers, and the PC's

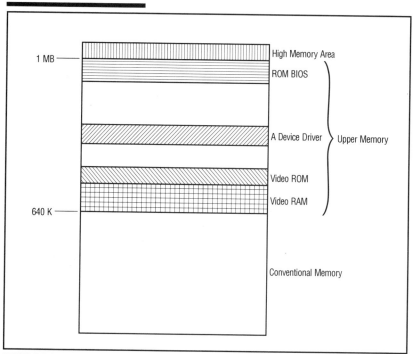

FIGURE 1.1: *A map of DOS memory*

ROM itself. What is more confusing, you will sometimes see it called *high memory,* which makes it easy to confuse with the *High Memory Area,* described next. You will often see, for instance, the terms High Memory, High RAM, and High ROM in the QEMM documentation; these refer to this area of memory. Figure 1.1 shows BIOS for one device (a hard-disk drive) occupying a slice of the UMA, typical for a simple configuration. Devices may also place RAM in this region for special purposes.

Video RAM   The portion of the memory map immediately above 640K is dedicated to video RAM, although how much is actually used depends on the current video mode. As mentioned, your memory manager may be able to free some of this memory to load your device drivers and TSRs. What is more, if you use

DOS MEMORY

DOS memory is the range of memory traditionally available to PC processors, operating systems, and software, even if you are using the earliest PCs with their 8086 or 8088 processing chips. It includes space for RAM as well as ROM and is divided into two main areas: conventional memory and upper memory.

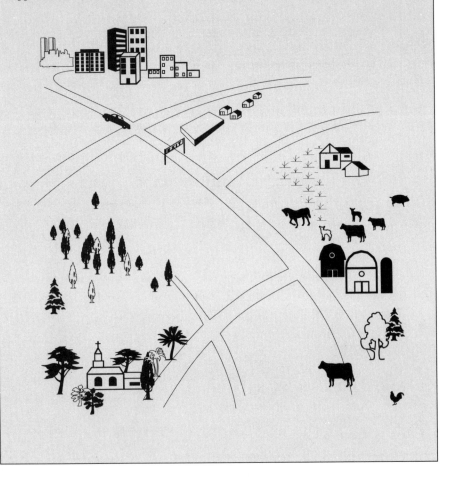

DOS memory is like a metropolitan area: The central city (with the very low numbered addresses) has the police station, the courts, and city administration buildings, surrounded by tightly packed businesses, residences, and parking garages (conventional memory). You pass a park and reach a video emporium and you're past the city limits; then you drive past blocks of open fields punctuated by an occasional subdivision or farm (upper memory). The last suburb is a small hamlet known as high memory—this may or may not be part of the metropolitan area, depending on whether the A20 bus line reaches it. (You'll learn more about the A20 line in the next chapter.) Beyond high memory are the exurbs and the countryside, known as extended memory; more on this region follows later.

text mode exclusively, the manager may be able to appropriate the first big chunk of the buffer (which is dedicated to graphics mode) and add it to conventional memory, giving you more than 700K for your applications.

Video ROM   The small area above the video buffer is available for video adapters (EGA, VGA, or later) to insert their own BIOS code. The routines will then be here that are actually used when DOS or an application makes a call to your PC's ROM BIOS for a video function.

The ROM BIOS   The size of the ROM BIOS may vary from one machine to another, but it typically occupies two slices of address space near the top of the UMA, beginning at about 980K.

Figure 1.1 shows empty spaces above and below the hard-disk code. These separate areas of address space are known as *upper memory blocks* (UMBs). They can be filled with RAM and made available for your TSRs (terminate-and-stay-resident programs) and some other programs by a process known as *remapping*, described later in this chapter.

The High Memory Area

The High Memory Area (HMA) is a bonus space available on most 80286 or later PCs. It exists because of a quirk in the design of Intel CPUs: DOS and PC applications are actually able to use a chip's internal registers to refer to almost 64K more memory (16 bytes short of 64K) than an 8086 or 8088 CPU can address.

> **NOTE** ⟩⟩
>
> *An internal register is a small storage area used to manipulate data or to form a memory address.*

When a memory manager activates the 21st address line on an 80286 or later chip, this memory becomes usable. You will see this line referred to in documentation as the *A20* line (the first line is called A0), and it must be activated by a special device driver included with DOS 5 (HIMEM.SYS) or built into QEMM or 386MAX.

You can load much of DOS 5 itself into the HMA, making more conventional memory available for your applications. Alternatively, the DESQview operating environment is often placed in the HMA. You will learn how to make best use of this area in the course of this book.

The HMA marks the beginning of extended memory, the region beyond the standard DOS limit that is available only to 80286 or later CPUs. Extended memory and how to use it make up one of the main topics of Chapter 2 of this book.

Focus on Conventional Memory

Figure 1.2 takes a closer look at conventional memory, with its typical uses. Like the previous figure, this one begins with address 0 at the bottom. This figure should give you a sense of the

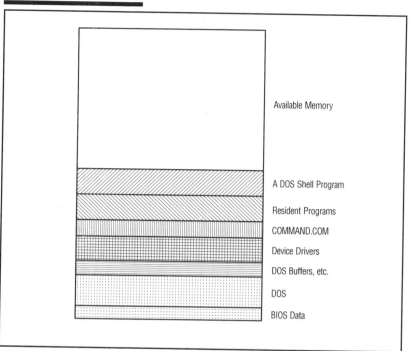

FIGURE 1.2: *A map of conventional memory*

phenomenon known as "RAM cram." Exactly where each element begins in memory depends on numerous factors, but this will give you a notion of the demands on memory.

✗ The lowest part of memory is a data area, a scratch pad for your PC's ROM BIOS, which includes such things as a record of your current machine configuration (about 2K).

✗ DOS's own internal routines and data areas appear next (about 60K in DOS 5.0 when not loaded high).

✗ The next block of memory contains elements such as *file handles* (created when DOS executes the FILES line in your CONFIG.SYS file) and *disk buffers* (the standard cache memory for faster disk I/O (input/output) that you size by using the BUFFERS line in CONFIG.SYS). You may choose to instruct DOS 5 to load the buffers in high memory instead, by using the DOS=HIGH line.

✗ Next come software device drivers that you designate in CONFIG.SYS, such as ANSI console drivers, RAM disks, and disk caches (demands for memory vary greatly).

✗ The resident portion of COMMAND.COM, the standard DOS program that interprets what you type at the DOS command line, comes next (about 5K with DOS 5.0).

✗ Next come any resident programs, or TSRs (usually activated when you press a hot key) that you have loaded using AUTOEXEC.BAT. There are all sorts of TSRs on the market; examples are Borland's SideKick program and various screen capture programs, like HotShot (demands for memory vary greatly).

✗ The example supposes that you are using some sort of menu-driven shell program designed to simplify life with DOS, such as the Norton Commander. The shell is loaded above the TSRs, starts running, and probably remains in memory while you use it to summon one or another application.

✗ When you "point and shoot" to start an application from the shell, the application has whatever is left of conventional memory to work in.

When you think of how demands on conventional memory are proliferating, you can see what a help it would be move some of these memory hogs somewhere else than conventional memory, such as into reserved memory above the 640K limit. This is one of the tasks of a competent memory manager like QEMM or 386MAX.

MEANS OF MANIPULATING MEMORY

You may wonder how it is possible to move, say, a TSR program or a set of disk buffers into an address space where no memory is found. The ability of a memory manager to do this relies on an ability of 80386 and later chips to *map* memory to any address. This simply means that the CPU can use internal tables to place any memory in your machine anywhere within its address space (but not overlapping other memory), using a special mode available to 80386 and i486 chips. With earlier chips, the location of memory in the address space was dictated by its physical position in the machine.

The ability to remap memory opens several possibilities to the memory manager.

Filling Upper Memory

You can also fill empty UMBs (upper memory blocks) from extended memory. Although DOS programs have been designed to operate in conventional memory, many TSRs and device drivers will run happily from a UMB.

Note that, if you buy a 386 or later PC with 1MB installed, 384K of memory will initially be mapped to the space above the DOS limit. This memory will be available for remapping to the upper memory area. If your PC's BIOS doesn't handle this remapping, QEMM or 386MAX can accomplish it.

Sorting

Memory in your system may vary in speed of access. QEMM or 386MAX will optionally test the speed of memory in your system and map the fastest memory to the lowest addresses, where it will be most heavily used.

REMAPPING

Mapping, obviously, is associated with maps—it means representing some terrain in a new medium. A systematic correspondence is established between one set of things and another. For instance, a number in a memory location or a CPU register can represent a location in a computer's memory where data or further instructions can be found. In the original PC, there was a simple one-to-one mapping between the number and the electrical location of memory in the PC, which is a one-dimensional continuum. The 80386 processor, however, can effectively shuffle memory to allow a given number to address any block in memory. Here, references to memory are virtualized, that is, they no longer refer literally to physical locations but are one step removed from them. This ability creates a lot of flexibility, including the ability to map the fastest memory to the lowest part of the memory map, where it will be most heavily used.

A memory manager can rearrange memory as you might rearrange the furniture in a room for different purposes, like for dinner and then dancing. Keep in mind, though, that this remapping is virtual and from a software point of view, memory remains physically in place as always.

ROM Shadowing

ROM is much slower to access than RAM, typically by a factor of about ten. Your memory manager can take advantage of the speed of RAM to make BIOS routines, and thus your applications, run faster, by a process of remapping in which it does the following:

✗ Copies the contents of the ROM BIOS, video ROM, or other ROM to a chunk of RAM that is the same size

✗ Remaps the original ROM to the high end of the address space, well out of the way

✗ Remaps the RAM bearing the BIOS instructions to the address space formally occupied by the ROM

The remapped RAM in this case is known as *shadow RAM*. Note that some PCs have ROM shadowing built into their BIOS. Typically, the PC BIOS will allocate 384K of unused RAM (which equals 1MB minus conventional memory) to RAM shadowing. Memory managers can reclaim any of this RAM that is not actually used. If your PC's BIOS leaves any ROM unshadowed, you can instruct your memory manager to pick up the loose ends.

Stealth

Stealth is Quarterdeck's name for a set of techniques currently featured in QEMM for getting double duty out of a range of memory addresses. For instance, BIOS instructions may be stored in extended memory and copied back to upper memory only upon demand. The original address range of these instructions is made available to hold TSRs or other programs. Because of the time required for copying alternate sets of data and instructions into memory, and because of occasional compatibility problems, stealth techniques are best used only when other DOS memory is exhausted.

Numbering Memory

In studying your memory manager's documentation or using programs like DOS's MEM, Quarterdeck's Manifest, or 386 to the Max's ASQ, you will come across hexadecimal numbers referring to memory addresses. These numbers (which use the letters A to F as digits for numerical values from 10 to 15) are convenient shorthand for binary values—each digit represents four binary digits. Thus, they tend to yield nice, round numbers for a PC, where powers of 2 reign supreme. They are also readily translated into decimal values.

In this book, you will see decimal equivalents for hexadecimal values from time to time. You can also refer to Appendix A
for a quick account of how to interpret hex numbers and translate
them to their decimal equivalents.

PROBING MEMORY

You can get a quick snapshot of memory usage under DOS 5 by
simply entering MEM at the DOS prompt. The output may look
something like this:

```
655360 bytes total conventional memory
655360 bytes available to MS-DOS
584016 largest executable program size

7864320 bytes total EMS memory
4128768 bytes free EMS memory

7340032 bytes total contiguous extended memory
      0 bytes available contiguous extended memory
4063232 bytes available XMS memory
  64Kb High Memory Area available
```

Line by line, this shows you the following:

✗ The amount of conventional memory installed in your PC.

✗ The amount of conventional memory available to DOS,
which normally matches the total memory installed.

✗ The amount of memory free at the time MEM was executed (conventional memory minus that occupied by
DOS, resident programs, and so forth).

✗ The amount of expanded memory. In the sample MEM output, the expanded memory is really extended memory that has been converted by a memory manager (QEMM) and made available as EMS (Expanded Memory Specification) memory. Expanded memory is described in the next chapter.

✗ The amount of expanded memory not currently in use.

✗ The amount of extended memory installed (total memory minus conventional memory and memory used for functions like ROM shadowing).

✗ The amount of raw extended memory not currently being administered by a memory manager. This figure is 0 because QEMM has been set to administer all memory.

✗ The amount of XMS (Extended Memory Specification) memory available. XMS is a standard for administering extended memory, described in Chapter 2. The figure is close to that for EMS available because QEMM will normally allocate its memory pool as EMS or XMS on demand.

✗ Whether the HMA is available, that is, not occupied by DOS or some other program.

MEM has options for further detailing memory contents; for instance, enter MEM /C (for CLASSIFY) to see how much space in conventional memory is occupied. This variation of the MEM command conveniently includes columns of exact decimal numbers, rounded numbers in kilobytes, and hex numbers for program sizes.

You now have a basic understanding of how your PC uses memory and especially how memory is organized under DOS. The following chapter will introduce what lies beyond the DOS 1-megabyte limit: expanded and extended memory. After that, we will take a closer look at the further possibilities offered for memory under two popular operating environments: DOS 5 and Microsoft Windows.

CHAPTER TWO

RECALLING

MEMORY

There have been two great breaches in the wall of DOS memory limits: *expanded memory* and *extended memory.* If there were any simple mnemonic device to help remember which is which, everyone would know it by now. As it is, perhaps you can remember that expanded memory is obsolescent, a vestige of the 8088 CPU and the software that evolved around it. Extended memory, on the other hand, is the future, toward which all PC operating systems, environments, and major applications are evolving. This chapter will take a look at these schemes for making more room available to applications.

UNDERSTANDING EXPANDED MEMORY

Expanded memory was a makeshift to make more memory available to 8088 processors using their 1MB address space; it was devised when users began devising huge databases and spreadsheets that could no longer be contained within 640K. It was implemented using special add-on cards inserted in PCs that could dole out RAM from their own banks on demand.

So what is expanded memory? In its simplest form, the expanded memory board appropriates a block of upper memory when your PC boots. When you start an application that uses expanded memory (and load, say, a spreadsheet), it requests that the board copy its data into the board RAM—this is the process of allocating some of its store of expanded memory. Then, when the application is ready to work with some of the data, it requests that the board copy the data into an upper memory block. This act of making a block of data accessible is called *paging,* the particular set of data is called a *page* of the total data, and the upper memory block is called a *page frame.*

Note that the application must be aware of expanded memory, know how to communicate with the board, and keep track of what pages particular ranges of data occupy. A software device driver called the Expanded Memory Manager (EMM) aids the application in carrying out the details. The EMM is a file supplied with the memory board and installed using the CONFIG.SYS file.

Expanded memory had its beginnings in various proprietary devices, such as Tall Tree Systems' JRAM board. Soon thereafter, in 1985, Lotus, Intel, and Microsoft jointly developed a standard for expanded memory known as LIM EMS (Lotus-Intel-Microsoft Expanded Memory Specification). The first version to achieve prominence was LIM EMS 3.2. LIM EMS created a 64K page

EXPANDED MEMORY

Keep in mind that expanded memory involves an area called the page frame, usually located in upper memory, which an application can request be supplied with blocks of data supplied from elsewhere: originally from special RAM on the expanded memory card, but also, in the case of emulated expanded memory, from extended memory (described later) or even from disk. What this process asks of your memory manager and, in some cases, of you is that sufficient space exist in upper memory to create this page frame without conflicts with other users of upper memory. It also asks that enough extended memory be available to meet the requirements of your applications (those that use expanded memory) for storing data.

In Chapter 1, we compared DOS memory to a metropolitan area, in which conventional memory (the lower 640K, normally filled with RAM) was within the city limits, and upper memory (the remaining 384K) was the suburbs. In this analogy, the EMS page frame is a park in the suburbs, accessible using the DOS city bus lines. The origins of the park flora and fauna would vary: For an actual EMS board, they would come from the exotic land of the RAM populating the board. In the case of emulated EMS, they would come from a region in extended memory or from a disk drive.

frame in expanded memory that could hold four separate 16K pages of expanded memory at a time, as shown in Figure 2.1. Any given application requesting RAM was assigned a unique identifying *handle* and was prevented from using memory assigned to another program. The board itself could contain up to 8MB of RAM. Besides this, the expanded memory board could use some of its RAM to backfill the motherboard to a full 640K, if the PC came supplied with a smaller quantity. Some boards were sold that could be configured as EMS memory or as extended memory (described later) by means of a switch setting.

EMS became popular not only with spreadsheet developers but also with producers of numerous products, including network drivers, RAM disks, disk caches, and printer spoolers.

In late 1987, the original partners released the current (and perhaps last) form of EMS, which is version 4.0. It maintains compatibility with its predecessor and also incorporates features from a formerly competing product known as AQA EEMS (AST/Quadram/Ashton-Tate Enhanced Expanded Memory Specification, after its joint developers). EMS 4.0 allows variations in the size of page frames, allows them to be placed practically anywhere in conventional memory, and allows program code to be run from them, aiding the work of multitasking environments such as DESQview. It also allows for use of up to 32MB of RAM. Few applications, however, make use of the advanced capabilities of this specification.

EMS Emulators

Not long after the introduction of EMS boards, developers accomplished software-only emulations of EMS, using only extended memory and special drivers. (A few early products used disk drives to emulate expanded memory, an extremely slow process but better than nothing if you absolutely needed the space.) These products were also sometimes known as *LIMulators*

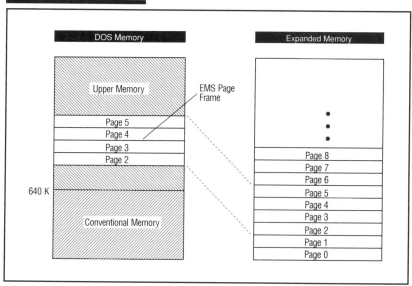

FIGURE 2.1: *Expanded memory in action*

after the LIM specification. Many of these products implemented something less than the full EMS 4.0 specification, or did so imperfectly. With the advent of the 80386 CPU, EMS emulation became straightforward, because this chip has built-in means for paging memory.

Modern memory managers like QEMM and 386MAX include all the features of LIM EMS 4.0 emulators, incorporating the function of the Expanded Memory Manager and allocating expanded memory out of their pool of RAM.

UNDERSTANDING EXTENDED MEMORY

Extended memory is simply RAM that lies beyond the 1MB address range of the 8086 or 8088 CPU, as you can see in Figure 2.2.

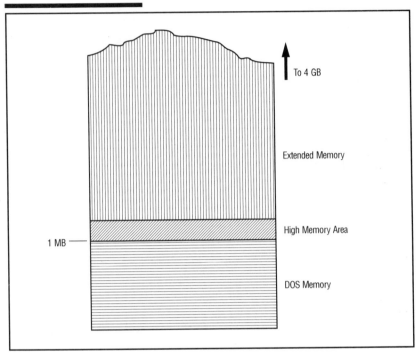

To 4 GB

Extended Memory

High Memory Area

1 MB

DOS Memory

FIGURE 2.2: *Extended memory*

Remember that the 80286 chip, with its 24 address lines, can address up to 16MB of memory, and the 80386 and i486, with their 32 address lines, can address up to 4GB of memory.

Real Mode vs. Protected Mode

When you power up an 80386 or i486 chip, it comes up in a mode in which it emulates an 8088, known as *real mode*, and in which it can address only 1MB of memory, just as the earlier CPU can. These newer chips were designed this way to make it possible to run DOS, which was heavily entrenched in the PC world and inextricably tied to the 1MB of conventional memory. To address

EXTENDED MEMORY

Unlike expanded memory, extended memory is just the native memory available to an 80286 or later processor. In terms of DOS, extended memory is that lying beyond the DOS limit of 1MB. In terms of the RAM in your PC, any RAM beyond 640K (minus RAM used to backfill conventional and upper memory, or used as shadow RAM) becomes extended memory, which must be addressed by leaving DOS and using the processor's protected mode of operation. (There are a couple of minor exceptions, including the High Memory Area.) To put it another way, extended memory is all your system RAM minus what DOS and the BIOS have allocated as conventional memory or used for other purposes.

Using our previous analogy of DOS memory as a metropolitan area, extended memory is the open country beyond that area, no longer reachable by the (20) metropolitan bus lines. The extent of the region depends on the address range of the processor, or on how much RAM is actually installed.

more memory than an 8088, the later chips must—with certain minor exceptions—be placed in a special mode of operation, known as *protected mode.* In protected mode, all the chip's address lines are activated, and it can use its full potential address range.

Where do these two modes get their names? In an 8088 chip or a later chip running in real mode, addresses are formed using the sum of two registers (temporary storage locations inside the CPU)—the value in one register is multiplied by 16 (which is 2^4) and then added to the other value. This is the trick that allows use of the High Memory Area (HMA), described in Chapter 1—the value that can be formed is about 64K greater than 1MB. The first register clearly, can only see memory in 16-byte jumps. This register is known as a *segment register,* and the 64K of memory that it can refer to is a segment. The second, or more finely calibrated, register points to a position in memory within that segment known as an *offset.* Real mode gets its name because the value in the segment register refers *directly* to an actual memory location.

In protected mode, however, the 24-bit or 32-bit segment register refers to an entry in a table describing a location in memory rather than directly to an address. The existence of this table allows an operating system to inspect applications' references to memory and reject any that aren't legitimate; this is what makes protected mode protected. At any rate, a chip can see beyond 1MB (plus, sometimes, about 64K) only in protected mode, with only marginal exceptions.

As you can see, any DOS software that uses extended memory must be able to switch from real mode (the world that DOS knows) to protected mode (where it can get at the extra memory) and back again. This is a tricky process, especially with an 80286 chip. For a long time after extended memory became available, only VDISK, the RAM drive program supplied with DOS 3.0 and 3.1, had this capability. Over time, numerous applications and utilities have used extended memory, whether as a simple pool of RAM for data storage or as a complete environment to operate within.

REAL AND PROTECTED MODES

Real mode and protected mode are states that your PC's processor (286 or later) can assume, and they affect how the processor addresses memory. In real mode, your processor functions like the 8088 or 8086 chips that were found in early PCs; the CPU is bound by the 8088's limitations, including its 1MB address space. This limit is necessary for DOS to work. Protected mode allows access to the full address space available to the processor: 16MB for an 80286 or 80386SX, 4GB for an 80386DX or later. Unlike real mode, protected mode allows an operating system to control access to memory. Such control is important in multitasking systems, where multiple applications may be contending for computer resources. In the DOS world, memory managers use protected mode to reach and manipulate extended memory. They can then use this memory as a pool to allocate space for disk caches, expanded memory, and so forth.

The 80386 and later processors include a special submode of protected mode called *virtual* 86, or V86, mode. The processor creates a complete simulation of an 8086 processor, allowing DOS and DOS applications to run normally. However, the complete memory management tools of the 80386 processor remain online, behind the scenes, allowing the memory manager to use the processor's page tables to work with memory directly, paging memory, remapping memory, and protecting access to memory. Your memory manager operates your PC in this mode whenever you have set it to fill or sort conventional or video memory, to map parts of upper memory, or to provide expanded memory—that is to say, usually.

> Protected-mode addressing differs from real-mode addressing in referring to a location in extended memory rather than DOS memory and in referring to it indirectly, through a designated table entry. The two envelopes shown in the illustration reflect these distinctions—the first has an urban address (like DOS memory) and refers to a literal location, regardless of who owns it, whereas the second has a rural address (like extended memory) and a named addressee. Thus, a protected-mode memory address must bear the name of its holder and cannot be used by just anyone.

Standards for Extended Memory

Extended memory was the wild West for a time, as programs attempted to grab blocks of memory for themselves through simple means—VDISK was an example. Fortunately, several standards have emerged that allow memory managers to dole out memory as available and to arbitrate among competing applications. Less fortunately, these various standards are not easily reconciled, making it difficult to design a memory manager that can handle them all satisfactorily.

The Extended Memory Specification (XMS)

The Extended Memory Specification (XMS) was set out in 1988 by Microsoft, Intel, AST, and Lotus to provide a structured means of access to extended memory for real-mode DOS programs. Actually, the XMS is not restricted to extended memory, but covers three areas:

✗ Upper memory blocks, the top 384K of DOS memory, described in Chapter 1

✗ The High Memory Area, the first 64K of extended memory, which can be reached from real mode

✗ Extended memory proper, which is any RAM in the system beyond 1088K, and which can be divided into blocks and allocated

The XMS places control of these areas under a memory manager. Applications can then request allocations of memory from these areas just as they do from conventional memory. In DOS 5, the XMS functions are encapsulated in the driver called HIMEM.SYS, as you will read in the next chapter. When you use QEMM or 386MAX, the memory manager assumes these functions. One of the great feats of these memory managers (and one of their significant advantages over DOS 5) is that they can control a single pool of extended memory and dole out blocks of it as EMS or XMS memory upon request.

Most current programs using extended memory do so through the XMS interface. If you have a program that tries to grab raw extended memory, you may have to set up your memory manager with special options, as you will read.

DOS Extenders

Some PC applications have attained such a level of complexity that they need the wide-open spaces of extended memory to run (to run at their best, or even to run at all), not just to hold data. Familiar examples include Windows 3, Paradox, AutoCAD, and some popular programming environments. For this reason, developers have devised sophisticated systems known as *DOS extenders*. Typically, a company marketing a PC application licenses a DOS extender to extend these capabilities to its product, so, when you buy the product, you get the extender along with it.

When you start your application, this (simplified) series of steps happens:

1. The extender loads into conventional memory and runs like a regular program.

2. It receives an allocation of extended memory, switches to protected mode, sets up a complete DOS-like environment in extended memory, and loads the application proper into it.

3. As the application runs, the extender resolves all the application's calls to the operating system, either by handling them itself or by switching back to real mode and passing on the requests to DOS or the ROM BIOS.

DOS extenders may create a more DOS-like 16-bit environment or may run as 32-bit systems that exploit the 80386 or i486 chips to the fullest, but this makes little difference from the consumer's point of view, apart from operating efficiency. Like other users of extended memory, early DOS extenders (generally made by specialized companies like Phar Lap Software) each tended to assume that they were the only game in town and so were incompatible. Now, DOS extenders have ranked themselves under two competing standards, abbreviated VCPI and DPMI.

PROTECTED-MODE OPERATION

DOS extenders use DOS as a launching pad to lift demanding applications into the realm of extended memory and the advanced processing capabilities of the 80386 or i486 chip. The protected-mode application remains tethered to DOS and real mode for services such as access to devices. DOS extenders rely on your memory manager to receive an allocation of extended memory to run your program.

Protected-mode operation can be compared to a trip to the country (extended memory) for your application. You must ultimately return to the city (DOS), and you may have to make runs back into town for needed supplies (device access). Protected-mode operating systems such as Unix, however, are like living in the country and living off the land as a native of an advanced Intel processor's native mode, because the limitations of real mode, such as the 1MB limit, are then completely irrelevant.

The VCPI Standard The Virtual Control Program Interface (VCPI) standard was devised by Phar Lap and Quarterdeck in late 1987 to allow protected-mode programs (used with DOS extenders) to coexist with expanded memory managers and with each other. Basically, VCPI sets up the DOS-extended application as a VCPI *client,* which requests extended memory services, and sets up the memory manager as a VCPI *server,* which makes the extended memory available. This makes VCPI one more complex task for the memory manager to support.

The DPMI Standard The DOS Protected Mode Interface (DPMI) is chiefly a Microsoft invention, currently used in Windows 3 and in some programming environments from Microsoft and Borland. It was designed to support multitasking better than VCPI does. Like VCPI, DPMI works in terms of a client/server model.

Note these points:

✗ Windows 3 uses DPMI when in 386 enhanced mode (where it runs as a protected-mode program), but it virtually takes over your PC in this mode and does not need your memory manager as a server.

✗ Most DPMI clients will fall back on functioning as VCPI clients when no DPMI server is available.

✗ A few programs, such as the Microsoft C version 7 development environment, must have a DPMI server.

FUTURE MEMORY

DOS extenders and environments like Windows and DESQview point the way forward toward PC operating systems that will leave DOS, real mode, and the limitations of 8088 chips behind and fully exploit the high speeds, wide paths, and vast address ranges of 80386, i486, and later CPUs. Of course, systems like these will render memory managers as we know them obsolete. Of the contenders, it is uncertain if any one system will prevail in the marketplace, and if so, which one. Unix, OS/2, and Windows NT have the highest profiles now.

Unix

Unix, a complete multitasking, multiuser operating system, was developed at AT&T Bell Laboratories in 1969. Its viability today is testimony to the fundamental strengths of the original design. However, its vaguely "techie" mystique has limited its acceptance in business, even though its first major application was for word processing in an ordinary office pool at Bell Laboratories. Thus, you are still most likely to encounter Unix today at a university, research institute, or corporate R&D lab.

Although simple by the standards of mainframe computer operating systems, Unix makes heavy demands on a PC's processing power, memory, and storage, which could not be adequately met before the advent of the 80386, cheap RAM, and high-capacity disk drives. Its requirements for RAM and disk space still seem like over-kill for most single users of stand-alone PCs.

Unix's portability across various machine environments may also, paradoxically, have limited its success in the broad commercial arena, since the kind of shrink-wrapped, ready-to-use software that PC and Mac users, for instance, have come to expect usually can't be taken from one kind of computer running Unix and loaded onto another. Compatibility problems may be lessening, however, as versions of Unix converge on a single standard and as graphics-based windowed environments based on the X Window system, with its close association with Unix, become more widespread. For instance, Quarterdeck has released DESQview X, an X Window environment that operates under

DOS but that will run any software strictly designed for X Window. Products like this one will help bridge the gap between DOS and Unix.

OS/2

OS/2 is an elegant multitasking PC operating system (though chiefly for single users) that has great promise as the successor to DOS but that has been hampered by factors in its design evolution and marketing history.

The first great blow to OS/2 was IBM's and Microsoft's decision to design the system around the 80286 CPU, with its inherent limitations. Among other things, this made it impossible for the system to run existing DOS software adequately (allowing no more than one DOS session at any one time), thus reducing its attractiveness to potential buyers who wanted to get the most out of their existing software. Also, new software designed expressly to take advantage of OS/2 has been slow to appear.

Marketing factors have placed OS/2 head to head with the evolving forms of Microsoft Windows, and the latter, although more primitive and weak in concept, has proven much more attractive to software developers and therefore much more rich in available applications. If and when popular applications appear for OS/2, however, this operating system may pick up steam.

Windows NT

Windows NT is expected to be what, in some ways, OS/2 should have been: a complete multitasking operating system capable of taking full advantage of protected mode on 80386 and later CPUs, as well as being transportable to other hardware platforms. When it appears, it will have the head start of being able to run most existing Windows programs with little modification, as well as newer, higher-performance programs designed for the new environment.

Now that you have a basic conception of extended and expanded memory, plus the picture of conventional memory you
gained from Chapter 1, we're back to the situation on the ground:
your PC and DOS, as they attempt to keep pace with this ever-
evolving software and hardware environment. The next chapter
will introduce how you can use DOS 5 to exploit upper memory,
extended memory, and expanded memory.

CHAPTER THREE

DOS

DOES

MEMORY

By taking a look at how DOS 5 handles memory, you'll gain a better appreciation for what a full-blown commercial memory manager can do. Also, this chapter will offer you some tips on handling memory that apply even when you are using a commercial memory manager, such as QEMM or 386MAX.

DOS 5 in itself does not offer the sophistication of QEMM or 386MAX, but it does include the basics to take advantage of a 386 processor. It has the following:

✗ A memory manager (HIMEM.SYS) that can handle extended (XMS) memory and the High Memory Area (HMA).

✗ An expanded memory emulator (EMM386.EXE) to provide LIM EMS 4.0 support as well as to handle requests for upper memory blocks (UMBs). For this last function, DOS 5 provides special commands to load device drivers (DEVICEHIGH) and programs such as TSRs (LOADHIGH) into upper memory.

In addition, here are two DOS 5 drivers that you may want to use, even if you are using QEMM or 386MAX:

✗ The RAM disk program RAMDRIVE.SYS

✗ The software disk cache SMARTDRV.SYS

There is also a command switch, DOS=, which affects how programs may be distributed between conventional memory on the one hand and upper memory and the High Memory Area on the other hand.

You can use QEMM or 386MAX effectively with Digital Research's DR DOS operating system—see Chapters 6 and 9 for some hints. We do not cover DR DOS's native memory-management utilities here.

INSTALLING DOS AFTER QEMM OR 386MAX

As you will see, it is simplest to install QEMM or 386MAX with the current version of DOS or Windows in place. This sequence allows the memory manager's installation program to make necessary updates to system files. Sometimes, however, you will need to update DOS or Windows with a memory manager version in place. This process is not difficult.

DOS 5's setup procedure will leave your current memory manager in place in CONFIG.SYS. Use a text editor or a word processor to view this file. If SETUP has made the first line of the file

```
DEVICE=SETVER.EXE
```

you can place this line after the line installing the memory manager (e.g., DEVICE=C:\QEMM\QEMM386.SYS), allowing SETVER to be moved into upper memory. You may also include the line DOS=HIGH to allow DOS to load into the HMA. Then, run the optimization program (OPTIMIZE for QEMM, MAXIMIZE for 386MAX) to adjust for the space requirements of the new version of DOS.

If you have an older version of QEMM or 386MAX, you should upgrade to the current version to take best advantage of DOS 5.

USING THE DOS MEMORY MANAGER, HIMEM.SYS

To use the DOS memory manager, you should *begin* your DOS configuration file, CONFIG.SYS, with the statement

```
device=c:\dos\himem.sys
```

Substitute the path to your copy of HIMEM.SYS if it is different.

> **TIP** ✕

> *You don't need the DOS memory manager HIMEM.SYS at all if*
> *you are using QEMM or 386MAX—in this case, it is best to*
> *remove the reference to it from your CONFIG.SYS file. You can*
> *make it ineffective by preceding the line that invokes it with REM:*
> *rem device=himem.sys. There is an exception in the case of QEMM*
> *users running certain Compaq systems or PCs with more than*
> *16MB of RAM; refer to your QEMM manual for details.*

If you used the DOS 5 installation program, it will have placed the device=himem.sys line in CONFIG.SYS for you. HIMEM.SYS has a number of options, which are listed in your DOS manual (you probably won't have to use any of them). Here are a couple of options of interest:

✗ The */hmamin=nn* switch tells HIMEM.SYS how many kilobytes of memory a program must request before it will be allowed to use the High Memory Area. (The range is 0K to 63K.) This makes the most efficient use of the HMA by leaving the least memory unused, since only one program can occupy the HMA. Any other programs requesting access to the HMA will be loaded into conventional memory instead. If you don't use this switch, the first program requesting the HMA will automatically get it. Since you will probably be loading DOS itself there using the DOS=HIGH line described next, you probably don't need this switch.

✗ The */machine=xxx* or */machine=nn* switch (abbreviated */m=xxx* or */m=nn*) covers incompatibilities in the ways various PCs make high memory (via the "line A20 handler") and extended memory available. The DOS 5 installation program probably picked the correct value for you if it was needed; for instance, if you have a PS/2

WHAT ARE CONFIG.SYS AND AUTOEXEC.BAT?

CONFIG.SYS and AUTOEXEC.BAT are two text files containing commands that DOS uses to configure itself when you boot up. Each command occupies one line in a file. To be effective, each file must be in the root directory of your boot drive, probably drive C.

CONFIG.SYS contains low-level commands (sometimes called *directives*) that set up your underlying system configuration. This function includes loading device drivers (such as a memory manager) and allocating basic resources for opening and reading files.

AUTOEXEC.BAT is a special batch file that is always processed at boot time. Thus, it contains commands that you might type at the DOS prompt, plus some special keywords to control how its contents are processed. It typically includes all the commands that you execute only once per session, such as setting up the DOS path and loading resident programs.

Although, strictly speaking, you can run DOS without either of these files, their absence implies that you are not using your PC to best advantage. For instance, without the BUFFERS directive in CONFIG.SYS (or without a disk cache), disk reads and writes will take place very slowly, and without the FILES directive, your applications may not be able to load enough files to run. In these cases, you should consult a good DOS handbook, such as *Mastering DOS 5*, Judd Robbins, SYBEX, 1991, to learn how best to set up these files.

machine, it will have inserted the option */m=ps2* or */m=2* (the equivalent numerical value). If you have difficulty, for instance, in loading DOS into high memory as described below, you should consult the file README.TXT that came with DOS 5 to see if your PC requires a special value for this option.

USING A TEXT EDITOR

In this book, you will often encounter the suggestion to use a text editor or word processor in nondocument mode to create or edit a system file. What is a text editor? It is a simple word processor that produces a document in a standard, universal format with normal line endings (a carriage-return character followed by a line-feed character) and no special codes added (DOS 5's MS-DOS Editor and Windows 3's Notepad are examples of widely available text editors.). A file produced by such an editor can be read by DOS, used as program source code, or sent over a telecommunications link via an ASCII file transfer. It can also be read by any other editor or word processor. The README files often included with your applications are always text files to allow all users to read them. This format is so useful that a word processor, too, will always include an option to save a file in "nondocument mode," as a "text file," or some such phrasing.

How do you know that you've successfully saved a file as text? A simple test is to use the DOS TYPE command. Enter

>type *filename*

and the file will appear on screen. If it has more lines than can fit on the screen, use the command

>type *filename* | more

and page through the file by pressing the spacebar.

You can try this, for instance, on your AUTOEXEC.BAT file; enter

>type c:\autoexec.bat | more

The text should appear on screen formatted properly, with no overwritten lines, no extra lines, no nonsense characters (although you may see a Ctrl-Z, which appears as a right-pointing arrow, at the end), and no beeping.

Whenever you are about to alter any system file (for DOS, Windows, or other software), it is a good idea to make a backup copy first. You can either

set your editor or word processor to make a backup copy on start-up or copy
the file manually from DOS before editing. You could make a copy of your
CONFIG.SYS file, for instance, by entering

copy c:\config.sys c:\config.bak

before proceeding to modify it. If anything goes wrong, you can issue the
COPY command again with the arguments reversed to undo your changes.

Remember to have a working floppy boot disk on hand to reboot your
system in case any changes make it impossible to reboot from your hard disk.

MAKING EXPANDED MEMORY AVAILABLE

The second step in setting up DOS 5 alone is installing the DOS Expanded Memory Manager, EMM386.EXE. Like HIMEM.SYS, this driver does double duty: It handles both expanded memory emulation and use of upper memory blocks. Also like HIMEM.SYS, EMM386.EXE is not helpful if you are using QEMM or 386MAX.
You invoke the emulator by placing the line

device=emm386.exe

with the file name preceded by an optional path specification, in CONFIG.SYS on a line preceding the DOS= directive. EMM386.EXE has a number of command-line options. The following are of most general interest; the rest are covered in your DOS 5 manual:

✗ Memory: a number from 16 to 32768 following EMM386.EXE specifies the number of kilobytes dedicated to expanded memory emulation (the default is 256K). The remaining extended memory may be used as XMS memory. Note this distinct drawback to the DOS 5 tools in comparison with QEMM or 386MAX: Using EMM386.EXE, you must apportion expanded and XMS memory at boot time; if you want to make more or less expanded memory available, you must edit CONFIG.SYS and reboot. The commercial memory managers work with a single pool of memory and make it available as EMS or XMS as requested.

✗ The RAM and EMS options: You use no more than one of these, which you type in as RAM or EMS. If you use neither, neither EMS nor upper memory will be available. If you include the word RAM at the end of the directive that loads EMM386.EXE, upper memory will be available, but no EMS page frame will be created. This gives you the greatest possible amount of upper memory, if you don't need EMS. If you include the word EMS instead, upper memory will be available, but 64 kilobytes of it will be used to create an EMS page frame.

✗ Other options cover such things as areas of memory to exclude, that is, to regard as unavailable for UMBs, and locations for the EMS page frame. Why to exclude memory and how to decide where to place the page frame are covered in detail in the chapters that discuss QEMM and 386MAX.

MAKING UPPER MEMORY AVAILABLE

The third line in your CONFIG.SYS file should be the DOS= directive. At least, this line, if it appears at all, must follow the line that invokes HIMEM.SYS or your memory manager, and it must follow the line invoking EMM386.EXE, if you use this driver.

This line offers three options:

dos=high

and

dos=umb

as well as the two arguments combined:

dos=high,umb

The form *dos=high* instructs DOS to load part of itself into the High Memory Area. This simple instruction can save you 40K or more of conventional memory. It is usable with HIMEM.SYS as well as with the commercial memory managers. The only reason not to use it is if you have another program that can make even more use of the HMA and thus offer you greater savings—DESQview is an example.

The form *dos=umb* makes sense only when you are using the DOS memory management utilities HIMEM.SYS and EMM386.EXE; that is, it doesn't work with QEMM and 386MAX. It enables use of the upper memory area, handled by EMM386.EXE, so you must use it if you want to move some of your TSRs or drivers to upper memory.

USING UPPER MEMORY

The fourth step in using DOS 5 alone is to actually load device drivers and resident programs into upper memory. Remember, the purpose is to conserve vital conventional memory by removing anything from it that you can. Devices are loaded into CONFIG.SYS on lines following the dos= line. The syntax is

devicehigh=[*drive:*][*path*]devicename [*your usual parameters to devicename*]

For instance, you would insert the line

devicehigh=c:\dos\ramdrive.sys 512 /e

to create a half-megabyte RAM disk in extended memory, placing the RAMDRIVE.SYS driver in upper memory.

In the case of resident programs, use the LOADHIGH command, which goes into your AUTOEXEC.BAT file. For instance, if you have a small pop-up calendar that you usually load by adding the command POP-CAL to AUTOEXEC.BAT, you would instead use the command

loadhigh pop-cal

If there were parameters to the original program, they would follow it on the line as usual.

TIP

You can reduce the memory occupied by resident programs by placing the commands that load them in AUTOEXEC.BAT before lines that create environment variables, such as the PATH and SET commands. The environment that is passed to the program is proportionately smaller. You can avoid the need for the DOS path by invoking the program using its full path—for instance, by typing **loadhigh c:\util\pop-cal***. If the program itself uses any environment variables, they must be set before you load the program. You can use the MEM /P command to see exactly how much space is occupied by each program and its environment space, shown as hexadecimal numbers.*

Deciding What to Load High

Compared with QEMM and 386MAX, DOS 5 offers very cumbersome means for determining what you can load into high memory.

LOADING HIGH

Loading high is simply the process of relocating device drivers and resident programs from conventional memory to upper memory. For this to work, you must have mapped RAM into available upper memory blocks. Most but not all drivers and programs are happy to work in upper memory, which is, after all, within the 1MB DOS limit. Using DOS 5 and nothing more, you can tell if a program has been successfully moved into upper memory by entering **mem /p | more.** Because this command lists programs loaded in conventional memory, if your program's name does not appear, you can assume that it was loaded high successfully.

Relocating a driver or resident program to upper memory is like relocating an office building lock, stock, and barrel from the central city to the suburbs—there, business proceeds as usual, but you have escaped the madding crowds downtown.

To see what you can load, with HIMEM.SYS and EMM386.EXE loaded, DOS=UMB set, and your device drivers and resident programs loaded as usual, run the DOS MEM command. The MEM /C (for *classify*) form is the easiest to interpret in this case. To view the results (which may exceed a single screen), enter the command in this form:

    mem /c | more

or enter

    mem /c > prn

to get a printed listing of memory contents. For instance, if MEM lists your POP-CAL program with a "Size in Decimal" of 4960 (4.8K) and a line appears reading

    Largest available upper memory block: 71632 (70.0K)

then, clearly, you can fit POP-CAL into upper memory using the LOADHIGH command.

Many resident programs need more memory to be loaded initially than they occupy when running—the code used to initialize the program is loaded higher in memory than the remaining code and data; once the program is initialized, this code is discarded, and the memory is returned to the system. Thus, the figure that you obtain for the program's size as it runs, using MEM or a utility supplied with a memory manager, will not reflect how much space the program needs to get started.

You may have to consult the program's documentation to find out how much room the program needs to load and to make sure that an adequate memory block is available. (As you will see, QEMM and 386MAX can make this determination themselves—another advantage they have.) You can tell DEVICEHIGH to allocate enough space by substituting the parameter

size=*nnn*

surrounded by spaces for the equal sign after DEVICEHIGH. The number *nnn* represents how many bytes are needed, as a hexadecimal number.

Making Sure of the Results

To see if your program was successfully loaded into high memory, reboot your computer with the edited system files and run the MEM command again. The program should no longer be listed in the contents of conventional memory, and the largest available upper memory block should be proportionally smaller.

Notes on Order of Loading

When you use DOS 5 alone, as each program is encountered in CONFIG.SYS or AUTOEXEC.BAT, it is loaded in the first upper memory block that will hold it. In general, it is most efficient to load the biggest programs first. You can achieve this effect only by placing them in the desired order, first in CONFIG.SYS and then in AUTOEXEC.BAT.

Sometimes, resident programs will insist on being loaded in a special order in memory in order to run. You can control this, on a cut-and-try basis, by entering them in that order in AUTOEXEC.BAT.

Some resident programs will not run in upper memory at all—sometimes because they need to find their own code in conventional memory. If a program refuses to run in upper memory, you may have to remove the LOADHIGH command that precedes it and let it run in conventional memory.

Be sure to keep a floppy boot disk handy in case one of your modifications causes your PC to hang. Prepare the disk using the DOS FORMAT command with the /s option. Copy your favorite small utilities, including a text editor, to it. Try booting from it and making sure it works before you have to depend on it to revive your system.

Too Much of a Good Thing?

When you have succeeded in freeing more than 576K of conventional memory, you may find that certain DOS programs refuse to run and you see instead the error message

Packed file corrupt

Some older programs incorporated an assumption that they would not be loaded in the lowest 64K of memory, which would be taken up with DOS and BIOS functions. For this reason, DOS 5 has provided the LOADFIX program, which will load a program above the 64K mark. To use this command, just put it before the name of your program, by entering

loadfix *programname usual parameters to your program*

You can easily incorporate this command in a batch file, which will include the line

@echo off

and then the revised command line. If you pass various parameters to your application, use this form of the command:

loadfix *programname* %1 %2 %3

Use as many of the % replacement variables as you have parameters to pass. Try naming the batch file after the command that starts the application, but place it in a directory that occurs earlier on your path than the application. Precede *programname* with the full path to the original application.

This method applies as well to systems set up using QEMM or 386MAX as to those using the native DOS memory management utilities.

MAKING THE MOST OF EXTENDED MEMORY

The remainder of this chapter consists of tips for using extended memory to speed up your operations. These ideas apply whether you are using a commercial memory manager or DOS 5 alone.

Use a Software Disk Cache

If you have ample extended memory, a disk cache will save you much time by speeding up reading and writing to your disk drives. To use the disk cache provided with DOS 5, for instance, you need only include this line in your CONFIG.SYS file:

```
device=c:\dos\smartdrv.sys 2048 /e
```

This assumes SMARTDRV.SYS is in a directory called DOS on your C drive. The value 2048 will allow creation of a 2MB cache. This is a good value if you have, say, 6 or 8 megabytes of RAM in your PC. Use a smaller value if you have less RAM. (But see tips for using Windows SMARTDrive in the next chapter for further guidelines on cache sizes. The Windows 3.0 version of SMART-Drive is nearly identical to the DOS 5 version, but the disk cache included with Windows 3.1 is much different—a resident program normally installed through AUTOEXEC.BAT.)

Remember that you may have to reserve RAM for needs such as a RAM disk, expanded memory, or programs run under a multitasking environment, such as DESQview or Windows. You can also create a larger cache, but you may note diminishing returns for larger values. The /e option places the cache itself in extended memory—you can place the SMARTDRV.SYS driver itself in upper memory using DEVICEHIGH or the corresponding programs included with QEMM or 386MAX.

Although you can place the cache in emulated expanded memory rather than directly in XMS memory, this will add needless overhead to caching activities and open the door to compatibility problems with environments like Windows.

NOTE ⟫

Many commercial disk caches are available that exceed the capabilities of DOS 5's SMARTDrive. The version of SMARTDrive included with Windows 3.1 is, in fact, a very fast cache.

Use a RAM Disk

A RAM disk addresses a slightly different set of needs than does a disk cache. It is a simulation of a physical disk drive carved out of RAM; as far as software is concerned, it is a real disk, but it runs far faster than any physical disk. Also, it is more volatile, since it ceases to exist when you reboot your PC or when power is interrupted. You should not use one for data too vital to be lost. What, then, is a RAM disk good for? Here follow some good uses and how to implement them.

First, how do you create a RAM disk? Using the driver provided with DOS 5, add a line like this to your CONFIG.SYS file:

```
device=c:\dos\ramdrive.sys 1024 /e
```

Use the path in your system to RAMDRIVE.SYS, and include this statement somewhere after the line that loads HIMEM.SYS or your memory manager. You can use DEVICEHIGH or an equivalent to load the RAMDRIVE.SYS driver itself into upper memory. The example will create a 1MB RAM disk in extended memory. You should determine a size for your RAM disk after considering how much space you need and how much available extended memory you have. Here are some possibilities:

✗ Create a temporary directory on the RAM drive. Many programs will read and write scratch files using a designated directory, and placing it in RAM will save time. Place these lines in your AUTOEXEC.BAT file (supposing that your RAM disk is drive E, it will get a letter one higher in the alphabet than the highest existing logical drive in your system):

```
md e:\tempfile
set tmp=e:\tempfile
set temp=e:\tempfile
```

✗ Run an entire application from the RAM disk. If you see the hard-disk light flash frequently as you use an application, it may be a good candidate. Place commands in AUTOEXEC.BAT to create a directory on the RAM drive and to copy the needed program files to that directory. Place that directory first in your PATH command for fastest access. Edit any environment variables ("SET *xxx*=") used by that application to the new directory.

✗ Place your favorite small utilities on the RAM disk. Create a permanent directory for them (say, C:\USEALOT). Place this line in AUTOEXEC.BAT:

```
copy c:\usealot\*.* e:\tempfile >nul
```

Add E:\TEMPFILE to the beginning of your path as described.

✗ Copy COMMAND.COM from the root directory of your boot drive to the new directory on the RAM disk and make it effective by adding the line

```
set comspec=e:\tempfile\command.com
```

Since COMMAND.COM often must partly reload itself into conventional memory after a large application has run, this will speed your return to DOS when you exit.

✗ Run batch files from the RAM disk. DOS's COMMAND.COM reads, interprets, and executes batch files from disk line-by-line, which is time consuming. If you keep your batch files in C:\USEALOT as described in the previous example, you will find that they run much faster from the RAM drive.

MORE WAYS TO CONSERVE MEMORY

Here are some miscellaneous tips for conserving memory:

✗ Make sure that the FILES and BUFFERS lines in CONFIG.SYS are set no higher than necessary, as recommended by your application vendors.

✗ Go through your AUTOEXEC.BAT file and remove references to resident programs that you don't actually use, as well as obsolete SET commands and unused directories in your PATH.

✗ Gain an understanding of the DOS EXIT command and the process of "shelling out" from a program—that is, the sequence in which you temporarily leave the application suspended, use DOS, and then return by entering EXIT. Don't, for instance, start WordPerfect Office, shell to DOS, and then start another copy of Office while the original copy of Office and the extra copy of DOS remain in memory. Sometimes DOS users repeat this process until they run out of memory.

✗ Use options in your applications to use protected mode, extended memory, or expanded memory wherever possible.

✗ Use the latest version of DOS, which is compact and can be largely fit into high memory, as described previously.

✗ Load device drivers and resident programs into upper memory wherever possible, as described previously.

You should now have a feel for memory management as it comes out of the box with DOS 5. You'll be able to contrast DOS's approach to managing memory with the more sophisticated, capable, and helpful approaches taken by QEMM (Chapters 5-7) and 386MAX (Chapters 8-10). The next chapter takes up the special memory management requirements of a complex environment, Windows 3.

CHAPTER FOUR

WINDOWS

DOES

MEMORY

X

This chapter is an overview of the special memory requirements of Microsoft Windows. Even if you don't use Windows, however, you may find it worthwhile to scan this chapter for insights into using memory managers in support of large and complex operating environments.

Windows has put a new face on PC computing: multiple, movable windows, pull-down menus, dialog boxes, graphics-based screens. All these are now familiar features to Windows users.

Windows, however, has placed new stresses on the PC and the DOS environment. Windows has evolved into practically a new protected-mode operating system: It uses DOS as a launching pad and then takes advantage of extended memory and the protected-mode features of the 286, 386, and later CPUs to conduct multiprocessing (running more than one program at once) and to use the large expanses of memory needed by the complex functions that make a graphical environment usable. These stresses include special memory management problems that will be outlined in this chapter.

NOTE ≫

Look at Chapter 6 for information on QEMM and at Chapter 9 for information on 386MAX.

UNDERSTANDING WINDOWS MODES

As the PC has evolved, Windows has evolved along with it, to take advantage of improved hardware capabilities. Windows is able to operate in different modes to help make these advances while preserving compatibility with less powerful machines.

Versions of Windows through 3.0 included *real mode,* which operated under the native mode of the 8088 chip and its emulations. It could use an expanded memory card to supplement conventional memory.

The Two Modes

Windows 3.1 no longer includes real mode, but versions 3.0 and 3.1 have in common two modes that are based on the protected mode of 286 and later chips. These are called *standard mode* and *386 enhanced mode.* In both these modes, Windows loads itself in extended memory and operates in the protected mode of the CPU.

The clearest difference between the two modes lies in how Windows treats DOS applications. If Windows is running in standard mode, Windows returns to real mode (or V86 mode, if the PC was in that mode when Windows was started) to run a single DOS session; when you switch away from that session, it is suspended. Thus, you can run only one DOS session at a time, because only one instance of real mode is possible. (Windows cannot create a new virtual DOS session using standard mode because standard mode does not use the capabilities of the 386 processor.) Also, because functions such as video cannot be virtualized in real mode (that is, because Windows cannot intermediate between the program and the hardware), DOS applications must be given the entire screen rather than being run in a window.

When you start a DOS application in 386 enhanced mode, Windows places the processor in a virtual DOS session of Windows' own making. Because more than one V86 session is possible, more than one DOS application can continue running in the background after you switch away from it. Also, since Windows can virtualize access to hardware in this mode, it can run DOS applications in windows as well as arbitrate access to devices such as printers. Figure 4.1 illustrates the different ways that the two modes treat DOS applications.

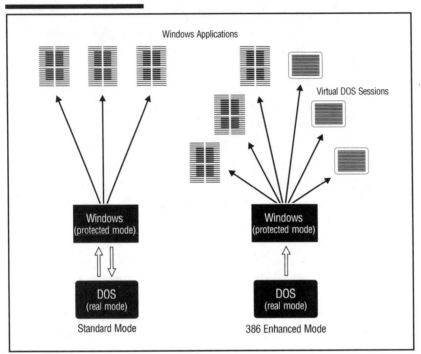

Windows Applications

Virtual DOS Sessions

Windows
(protected mode)

Windows
(protected mode)

DOS
(real mode)

DOS
(real mode)

Standard Mode

386 Enhanced Mode

FIGURE 4.1: *DOS and the two Windows modes*

Your memory manager can help you to make the most of Windows by managing conventional, upper, and extended memory most efficiently. When used with DOS, it performs functions that DOS's own memory manager cannot, such as placing TSRs in upper memory blocks most efficiently and making extended memory available as either EMS or XMS memory.

The memory manager serves Windows best in standard mode, where it acts as a VCPI server providing EMS and XMS memory as Windows requests. In 386 enhanced mode, Windows' own built-in memory manager basically takes over the system, and QEMM or 386MAX steps aside once Windows gets under way.

Protected and V86 modes, as well as VCPI, are described in Chapter 2 of this book.

Choosing an Operating Mode

When you start Windows 3.1, it will choose an operating mode automatically, on the basis of your hardware configuration. However, you can force Windows to start in standard mode by entering:

win /s

You can make it attempt to start in enhanced mode by entering:

win /3

Although Windows will always start in enhanced mode if it perceives that your hardware will support it, you may find that there are pluses and minuses to using either mode. Here are some reasons for using enhanced mode:

✗ You can run DOS sessions in the background—that is, while working actively with Windows applications—only in this mode.

✗ Similarly, you can run DOS programs in windows or reduce them to icons only in this mode.

✗ The Windows enhanced configuration yields a few more kilobytes of conventional memory for your DOS applications.

✗ Windows can read from and write to a hard disk at higher speeds on certain PCs.

✗ Enhanced mode improves access to virtual memory, that is, to disk space Windows uses to store applications or parts of applications when actual RAM is in short supply.

✗ If you want to supply expanded memory to DOS applications running under Windows, and that expanded memory is to come from a pool of converted extended memory (as opposed to an EMS board), you need enhanced mode.

Now, here are reasons for using standard mode instead:

✗ If you have a 286 computer, the features of the 386 processor are, of course, unavailable.

✗ You need at least a megabyte of extended memory available—*beyond* what your software cache, RAM disk, and other extended memory consumers are using—for extended mode even to start. This means that your PC must have at least about 2MB of total RAM. To do useful work with Windows applications in enhanced mode, you should have at least 4MB of RAM. (Note that both modes also need about 256K of free conventional memory to start.)

✗ If you want to use an EMS board to supply expanded memory to DOS applications, Windows will make the board available only if it is running in standard mode. (This is a consequence of switching back to real mode.) Remember, however, that it is always better to set the board to supply extended memory if that option is available. QEMM or 386MAX can then supply that memory as EMS or XMS as your programs demand.

✗ In general, Windows will perform about 20 percent more slowly in enhanced mode than in standard mode, because of extra overhead. This is often sufficient reason to choose standard mode, if you don't need enhanced mode for some reason.

✗ Memory management issues become trickier in enhanced mode, as you will see outlined later and detailed in Chapters 6 and 9.

✗ In some cases, you will not be able to use enhanced mode because of hardware incompatibilities—that is, because Windows takes direct control of more of your PC's hardware in this mode, not always successfully.

CHOOSING SUPPLEMENTAL PROGRAMS

As noted in Chapter 3, the DOS 5 memory management programs (HIMEM.SYS, EMM386.SYS, and the LOADHIGH and DEVICEHIGH commands) make up one system for handling memory, the QEMM package (QEMM386.SYS, QEMM.COM, the LOADHI and DEVICEHI commands, and others) makes up another, and the 386MAX package (386MAX.SYS, 386LOAD.SYS, 386LOAD.COM, and others) makes up a third. In general, you should use the programs from any one package as a set. Also, as always, you should obtain the latest versions of any of these packages to benefit from improvements and bug fixes.

Here are further notes for your Windows installation:

✗ By all means, upgrade your system to DOS 5. Using this latest version of the operating system will solve many Windows-related problems.

✗ Use HIMEM.SYS, EMM386.SYS, and LOADHIGH and DEVICEHIGH (note the fuller spelling of the commands) together. There is rarely reason to load HIMEM.SYS along with QEMM386.SYS and never reason to use DOS=UMB, EMM386.SYS, or the LOADHIGH and DEVICEHIGH commands with it. QEMM uses LOADHI and DEVICEHI.

✗ Windows includes versions of HIMEM.SYS and EMM386.SYS that are improved over the DOS 5 versions.

If you use these drivers, your CONFIG.SYS file should invoke them, including paths to your Windows directory, for instance

device=c:\windows\himem.sys

✗ Make sure that a file called WINA20.386 is present in the root directory of your boot drive. Otherwise, Windows may not run properly in enhanced mode. This file is used to handle contention between DOS and Windows for the High Memory Area.

✗ The Windows 3.1 version of SMARTDrive is much improved over the DOS 5 version, offering such advantages as write-back caching, where disk writes are delayed and combined. After installing Windows, you should make sure that the original invocation of SMARTDrive in CONFIG.SYS is commented out. The new SMARTDrive is a resident program, invoked in AUTOEXEC.BAT in a line such as this:

C:\WINDOWS\SMARTDRV.EXE

The line may include some parameters. Some hints on sizing SMARTDrive to your system appear below.

Windows on installation may invoke a small driver in your CONFIG.SYS file to *double-buffer* your disk drive. Bus-mastering controllers, such as SCSI controllers, may need this driver to maintain a fixed address in memory for read and write activity. This is because they address memory directly, bypassing the CPU. In 386 protected mode, the CPU may be remapping memory, rendering the address known to the disk controller obsolete without its knowledge.

Some newer SCSI (small computer system interface) controllers avoid this problem by adhering to a standard for memory access known as *Virtual DMA Services* (VDS) or by doing their own double buffering. If you use a SCSI controller and it was not

DELAYED WRITES

All disk caches work to speed reading from disks, for instance, by retaining recently read material or reading ahead. But some caches write whatever is requested to be written immediately, for greatest simplicity and data security. (This is called write-through caching.) Some more sophisticated caches may hold data until they are full or an interval has elapsed. (This is called delayed-write caching or write-back caching.) In this way, they can consolidate several write requests into a single operation, thus speeding writing. The loss in security is small, considering that writes are never delayed more than a few seconds. (How often do *you* save documents or spreadsheets you are working on to disk?) These caches will inevitably allow an optional parameter to turn off write delays.

A physical filing system in which you had to refile each document every time that you made a change in one of them might be very inefficient. You would probably prefer to keep the document at your desk until all changes were made, or until it seemed that no more changes were forthcoming soon.

supplied with a VDS driver, you should contact the manufacturer and find if one is available. By using one, you can avoid the need for double buffering and head off other potential compatibility problems. Few other disk drives do bus mastering. There are a couple of points to be noted here.

First, if Windows has placed a line like

```
DEVICE=C:\WINDOWS\SMARTDRV.EXE /DOUBLE_BUFFER
```

in CONFIG.SYS, and if, when you give the DOS command

```
smartdrv /s
```

all the lines in the "buffering" column on the far right read "no," you can remove this line from CONFIG.SYS and thereby speed disk accesses and save some memory. You can take the line out of effect most readily by prefacing it with the word REM and a space, using a text editor such as Windows' Notepad or a word processor in nondocument mode.

If a "yes" appears in the buffering column for one of the drives, you probably need double buffering. If a hyphen appears for one or more drives, and no "yes" appears, it is worthwhile to try removing double buffering.

Second, QEMM's OPTIMIZE command or 386MAX's MAX-IMIZE command may attempt to load the double-buffering device high, but it functions properly only when left to load itself high. If any language such as LOADHI precedes this line, you should edit it out so that the line begins "DEVICE=," with nothing preceding it.

Windows' SMARTDrive makes an excellent software cache for use with or without Windows in conjunction with HIMEM.SYS, QEMM, or 386MAX. A number of other cache programs are also usable, including Qcache, provided with the 386MAX package, Vcache from Golden Bow Systems, NCACHE, a part of the Norton Utilities, and SuperPCKwik.

The QEMM and 386MAX drivers may need special parameters to work with Windows enhanced mode. Most especially, the line that invokes QEMM in CONFIG.SYS should include three parameters,

DEVICE=C:\QEMM\QEMM386.SYS RAM NOVIDEOFILL NOSORT

to allow QEMM to fill upper memory for Windows' use and to prevent it from allocating memory in ways that conflict with Windows' expectations. For instance, if QEMM sorts memory by speed and then hands control over to Windows enhanced mode, QEMM's new mappings won't apply, and memory may be scrambled. (In the case of 386MAX, you may need to use the RAM= parameter, and to omit its SWAP= parameter, to avoid similar conflicts.).

You must have proper versions of special files (WIN-HIRAM.VXD and sometimes WINSTLTH.VXD for QEMM and 386MAX.VXD for 386MAX) to handle the orderly transfer of power from the managers to Windows enhanced mode, and you may have to try special techniques to avoid contention over video memory and other areas of upper memory. If you are using QEMM, you may need an additional driver file called MONOUMB.386 or MONOUMB2.386 for best handling of video memory under enhanced mode. You will read details on using these files in Chapter 6.

You should make sure that the EMS page frame is located in upper memory (which it should be by default) rather than in conventional memory.

You may need to use the reporting features of QEMM or 386MAX to resolve conflicts in use of upper memory, including problems with page frame location, other conflicts between Windows and your memory manager, and conflicts with undetected device ROM or RAM in upper memory.

Techniques for uncovering and resolving all these problems are covered in detail in Chapter 6 (for QEMM) and Chapter 9 (for 386MAX).

MAKING BEST USE OF MEMORY UNDER WINDOWS

Using Windows, with its heavy demands on memory, you soon grow aware of the trade-offs involved in memory management. With a limited amount of RAM, you will want to do these things, in descending order of priority:

✗ Provide enough memory for Windows itself, and enough memory to load your Windows applications and keep them in memory with a minimal use of virtual memory and disk swap activity.

✗ Provide memory for the applications' data, when the applications use EMS or XMS memory for storing data. Using your 386 memory manager, this memory will be provided by the memory manager out of its pool of converted extended memory.

✗ Create a software disk cache large enough to speed up disk activity substantially.

✗ Create a RAM disk large enough to handle temporary files generated by Windows applications.

Optimizing Conventional Memory

There are some trade-offs in making the most of conventional memory:

✗ You need a certain amount of conventional memory to load Windows itself (although its demands are moderate; most of Windows is loaded into XMS) and to load DOS programs that you invoke under Windows. What might not be obvious is that the amount of conventional memory left over once Windows is loaded is reflected in the amount available for DOS or a DOS application called under Windows, in either standard or enhanced mode. DOS sessions under Windows enhanced mode *inherit* the original DOS environment; a DOS session under standard mode occupies the original environment itself.

✗ If you make more conventional memory available by loading drivers and TSRs high, the difference is borrowed from extended memory, which you also need in abundance.

You might find it best to do an end run around the problem: Go through your CONFIG.SYS and AUTOEXEC.BAT files and remove any drivers and resident programs that you don't actually use under Windows. Most resident programs, in fact, either cease working when Windows is loaded or are better replaced by Windows utilities that you can display and manipulate in a window.

If you must run a DOS pop-up program, you can start it from within Windows, using the Program Manager's Run command on the File menu, an icon, or the File Manager. Also, you can run a pop-up in conjunction with a DOS application by creating a batch file that gives the successive commands to load the pop-up, run the application, and unload the pop-up (if such an option is available). You can then create an icon to run the batch file from the Program Manager.

NOTE

You can make better use of upper memory by setting devices to occupy contiguous space; this leaves large expanses of free address space open. These techniques are covered in more detail in Chapters 6 and 9.

If you work with both Windows and DOS, you may want to develop alternate boot configurations (alternate versions of CONFIG.SYS and AUTOEXEC.BAT) to give you the best possible setups for working with the programs. You could, for instance, load resident programs like SideKick under the DOS configuration only. Also, the best possible configuration for your memory manager (the best possible set of parameters when you run it) may look one way when you're running Windows and one way when you're not. See the section "Setting Up Alternate Configurations" at the end of this chapter for details on one way to make these configurations.

If you load TSRs under DOS and then run Windows, you can generally load them high or not, depending on whether it is more important to save conventional memory or extended memory. Note, however, that some TSRs that run fine with Windows when they are in conventional memory will cause problems when loaded high. If you have trouble starting Windows, you should try removing LOADHIGH (or LOADHI) commands from before the commands for these TSRs one by one and see if the problem disappears.

The same consideration applies to the DOS=HIGH line in CONFIG.SYS. Use this line to free additional conventional memory, or omit it to leave a bit more expanded or XMS memory available.

Windows needs sufficient DOS resources to run properly. You should make sure that your FILES line in CONFIG.SYS reads at least

    FILES=40

Alternatively, if you are running in 386 enhanced mode, and if you are using QEMM's FILES command to load some file handles high, the original directive in CONFIG.SYS should still read at least FILES=15, and there should be a total of at least 40 file handles.

Further optimizations are possible for Windows once you have a more detailed understanding of QEMM or 386MAX.

Optimizing Extended Memory

This section covers best use of extended memory and the devices that make their home there.

Windows does not use raw extended memory, but rather requests XMS memory from a memory manager. This means that, if possible, you should have your memory manager take control of all the extended memory in your machine. Don't use the EXTMEM or MEMORY parameters to QEMM to leave aside raw extended memory unless you absolutely require it for an older DOS program. (386MAX has no equivalent option.)

You can allocate parts of the extended memory available through the memory manager as a RAM disk and as a disk cache, leaving the rest available for Windows' direct use. Remember that Windows needs at least a megabyte of XMS free (after subtracting the needs of the disk cache and RAM disk, and the approximately 200K overhead for the memory manager) even to start in enhanced mode.

According to Microsoft, to perform useful work under Windows, you should leave at least 2MB of XMS free for standard mode and 2.5MB free for enhanced mode. Also, you need a minimum of free space on a drive to hold temporary files: 2MB for standard mode and 1MB for enhanced mode. The minimum size for a really useful disk cache is 512K, and you will see diminishing returns for any size above 4MB to 6MB. Table 4.1 suggests some cache and RAM disk sizes for a given amount of total memory in a system (as reported by the PC's power-on self test, or POST) running Windows in standard mode.

The numbers shown in the table are usually specified as multiples of a kilobyte (1024 bytes) or of half a kilobyte (512 bytes). The figures shown allow 1MB for conventional memory, upper memory, and ROM shadowing. If you run Windows in enhanced mode, the figures look like those shown in Table 4.2.

If you use the RAM disk to store other files, add their size requirements to the size for the RAM disk and to the total system memory requirement.

TABLE 4.1: *Collapsing directory levels*

TOTAL MEMORY (IN MB)	CACHE SIZE (IN K)	RAM DISK SIZE (IN K)
Less than 4	None	None
4	512	None
6	512	2048
8	2048	2048
12 or more	4096	4096

TABLE 4.2: *Suggested Cache and RAM Disk Sizes for Enhanced Mode*

TOTAL MEMORY (IN MB)	CACHE SIZE (IN K)	RAM DISK SIZE (IN K)
Less than 5	None	None
5	512	None
6	1024	1024
8	2048	2048
12 or more	4096	4096

Here is a further consideration: You may want to leave enough free memory available to hold those programs that you usually run at any one time in Windows. This avoids the delays involved in swapping programs to and from disk (using Windows' "virtual memory," described below). A hint: If you can switch from one running program to another using Alt-Tab, or any other means without the hard-drive light flashing, you have enough free memory available. Bring up each application in turn once so that Windows will attempt to load them all, and then bring them up in turn once again while watching the hard-disk light.

In Chapters 6 and 9, you'll learn how to check for free XMS memory using Quarterdeck's Manifest program or the Qualitas equivalent, called ASQ.

Setting Up a Disk Cache

Follow the directions for your disk cache to set it to the proper size. This is a possible command line for Windows SMARTDrive:

```
c:\windows\smartdrv a+ d e- /e:4096 2048 1024 /b:8192
```

c:\windows	Begin the line with the drive and path to your Windows directory. If Windows is on your DOS path, you may omit these. (If you use LOADHI or one of its relatives, of course, its name would appear first.)
a+ d e-	These are optional parameters for disk drives. By default, SMARTDrive read caches all floppy drives and read-and-write caches all logical drives (each drive letter represents a logical drive) on a hard disk. With this command, the letter *a* with the plus sign tells SMARTDrive to read-and-write cache the A drive, the letter *d* alone tells it only to read cache the D drive, and the letter *e* with the minus sign tells it not to cache the E drive at all. The B drive (if it exists), being a floppy drive and not included as a parameter, will be read cached only, and the C drive, being a hard drive and not included, will be read-and-write cached.

/e:4096	This parameter sets the size of the element: the number of bytes that will be read into the cache at once. Usually this parameter is omitted, because the default size of 8198 bytes is best.
2048 1024	These numbers represent disk sizes in kilobytes. SMARTDrive can accept one size for use under DOS, and another, smaller size for Windows. This is useful, because you will often have less extended memory to spare under Windows than otherwise. If you give just one number, it will be used both with and without Windows.
/b:8192	This number specifies the size (in bytes) of a read-ahead buffer. When you add this parameter, SMARTDrive will read this many bytes beyond the requested data. This increases the chances that the next requested data will already be in the cache, since read requests are often for sequential data. This parameter may be omitted; the default size of 16K is usually a good choice.

SMARTDrive accepts other parameters, which are mostly used by themselves. For instance, enter

smartdrv /s

at a DOS prompt for a summary of current SMARTDrive settings.

Setting Up a RAM Disk

A RAM disk is a simulation of a disk drive set up in RAM: You install a device driver (or, sometimes, a resident program) and tell it how large a disk you want. The driver appropriates a block of memory and creates all the necessary tables and other data structures to present the illusion of a real disk drive to other programs. (Some programs, such as disk-compacting utilities, recognize a RAM disk when they see one.) Drivers have been made that use DOS memory, raw extended memory, expanded memory, or XMS memory to create RAM disks.

The advantage of a RAM disk is speed; locations in RAM can be sought, read, and written very much faster than physical tracks on a disk. The disadvantages are that RAM disks disappear when your PC is rebooted and loses power, and that RAM disks are bound to be small, since RAM is much more expensive than disk storage space.

When one or more of your applications engages in heavy disk activity (as do many Windows applications), you can often save time as well as wear and tear on your hard disk by directing some of that activity to a RAM disk. You need only make sure that your permanent data wind up safe and sound on the hard disk itself. The steps below will show you some ways to make these things possible.

When you want to use a RAM disk to store temporary files, follow these steps:

1. Edit the command for your RAM disk to the size that you want to use. To set the DOS 5 RAM disk to 2MB, for example, use this line in CONFIG.SYS:

```
device=c:\dos\ramdrive.sys 2048
```

Use your path to DOS. Any additional parameters should be placed after the size. You can also use LOADHIGH.SYS or an equivalent command to load RAMDRIVE.SYS into upper memory.

2. Add the command

```
md x:\tempfile
```

to your AUTOEXEC.BAT file, substituting your RAM disk's drive letter for *x*.

3. Add the lines

```
set temp=x:\tempfile
set tmp=x:\etmpfile
```

to your AUTOEXEC.BAT file. The variable name TEMP to designate a temporary directory is a convention used by newer programs; many older programs look for a variable named TMP.

4. While you are editing AUTOEXEC.BAT, add COPY commands to copy small, frequently used utilities to the RAM disk. (You can copy them to the tempfile directory.) Be sure to leave enough space free for temporary files. Place the RAM disk at the beginning of your DOS PATH by editing PATH to read, say,

```
path x:\tempfile;c:\dos;c:\windows;[...]
```

where *x* is the drive letter for your RAM disk and the subsequent paths are whatever appeared there originally.

5. Reboot to put the settings into effect.

Avoid Expanded Memory

For best operation using Windows, set up your software to use XMS rather than expanded memory wherever possible. In particular, avoid using resident programs, disk caches, RAM disks, or network software that use expanded memory. In the case of common DOS 5 programs, this means that you must not use the DOS versions of SMARTDrive and RAMDrive with the /a switch.

If you don't need expanded memory, you can make more upper memory available to Windows enhanced mode by eliminating the page frame. You can do this with QEMM by adding the parameter FRAME=NONE to the line invoking QEMM386.SYS in

CONFIG.SYS. (Note, however, that you need a page frame to use QEMM's Stealth feature or to run DESQview.) For 386MAX.SYS, the equivalent parameter is NOFRAME. When upper memory is in short supply, Windows may need the added space to place its translation buffers in upper memory; otherwise, it must place them in conventional memory, making less space available for Windows itself and for your DOS programs running under Windows. The translation buffers are the means by which Windows moves data from protected mode to real mode and back when communicating with devices in your PC, such as disk drives.

If you need the page frame in DOS but not in enhanced mode, you can keep upper memory free by editing a line in the [386Enh] section of the SYSTEM.INI file, which appears in your WINDOWS subdirectory. This is an alternative to using FRAME=NONE or NOFRAME. Find the line ReservePageFrame and, using a text editor or word processor in nondocument mode, edit it to read

ReservePageFrame=false

Given this value, enhanced mode will still maintain a page frame if there is room both for it and the translation buffers in upper memory. Otherwise, it will eliminate the frame. (The page frame requires 64K of contiguous memory—the translation buffers, somewhat less.) If the value were set to true, the translation buffers, and sometimes the page frame itself, might be placed in conventional memory, at the expense of your DOS programs.

NOTE 〉〉

Remember that you can't eliminate the page frame if you run any DOS applications that use expanded memory under Windows. In this case, you should instead try to free more upper memory by not loading TSRs and by using the techniques described in Chapters 6 and 9.

Out of Memory?

If Windows flashes a message such as "Out of Memory" or "Insufficient Memory to Load Program," you may have alternatives to rushing out after more RAM or eliminating your disk cache and RAM disk. There are two immediate steps you should take to reduce the demands of Windows itself and its applications:

✗ Clear the Clipboard of its contents, which you can do by selecting the Clipboard Viewer from the Main window in Program Manager, pressing Del, and then selecting Yes to affirm that you want to delete the contents.

✗ Close any unneeded open applications, or reduce them to icons.

Further steps are changes to your Windows configuration and take effect after you restart Windows:

✗ Use the Desktop dialog box in Control Panel to set your wallpaper to NONE or to set a simpler pattern than your current one.

✗ Eliminate fonts that you don't use: Bring up the Fonts dialog box in Control Panel, select unneeded fonts, and click Remove. Do the same with other font managers that you use, such as Adobe Type Manager.

✗ Reduce your font manager's cache size. If you make this cache too small relative to the fonts that you use, however, operations that involve loading fonts may slow down appreciably.

You can see how much memory you have freed by selecting the About Program Manager option from the Help menu in Program Manager and looking at the amount of memory free.

Note also the amount of system resources free, given as a percentage in this window. At times, you will get out-of-memory errors even when there appears to be plenty of memory. These messages are usually traceable to a shortage of system resources, which are two areas of memory each at the disposal of two parts of Windows called GDI (Graphics Device Interface) and USER. GDI uses its area to store graphical screen elements, such as icons, windows, and toolbars. USER handles devices such as the keyboard and the mouse. Each of these two areas is limited to 64K no matter how much memory you have or how cannily you manage it. The About Program Manager box shows you the percent available of the more heavily used of the two areas.

You can ease your use of system resources by following these steps:

✗ Close Windows programs that you aren't using (or, at least, reduce them to icons). Each program grabs some resources.

✗ Eliminate screen elements that you don't need from running programs. This includes elements such as rulers, ribbons, and toolbars.

✗ In enhanced mode, run DOS programs full-screen instead of in a window. This way, no paraphernalia, such as title bars, become associated with them. You can set the program to run this way using the PIF Editor.

✗ Make sure that PIFs (program information files) for DOS programs give them no more conventional, EMS, or XMS memory than they need. (The Memory Requirements section in the PIF Editor window refers to conventional memory.) Check your program's documentation for the requirements.

✗ Remove program icons and program groups that you don't need or that are duplicates from the Program Manager.

✗ Avoid closing and restarting Windows applications repeatedly, because some applications may not release all their resources on exit, and so repeated runs can cause a steady depletion of resources.

Optimizing Virtual Memory

Virtual memory, like anything virtual, is a semblance: an illusion of RAM created from disk space. By using disk space as overflow RAM, Windows makes more memory available to applications.

How does Windows use virtual memory? When you start a new program and no more RAM is available, one or more of the applications already loaded are swapped to disk. What makes the illusion complete is that you can switch back to an earlier application and resume work from where you left off, without restarting it. It works only for applications that can be suspended, not for programs that are running in the background, like communications programs. Virtual memory takes different forms in standard mode and in enhanced mode.

VIRTUAL MEMORY

Virtual memory is the use of disk storage to hold the contents of memory. It is different from ordinary disk storage because parts of running programs or documents or other data items are not translated into or out of their normal file organization as they are written to or read from disk (although they are read or written to files). Instead, exact images of programs or data as they are found in memory are written.

You might compare virtual memory to stream-of-consciousness writing, in which you transcribe everything that comes to your head verbatim. If you could later read your jottings and resume thinking exactly what you were thinking before, this would be true virtual memory.

Virtual Memory in Standard Mode

In standard mode, Windows creates a swap file for each application to be used as needed. (These files are known as *application swap files*.) The file will be created, in order of preference, in the directory designated by the SWAPDISK setting in your SYSTEM.INI file, in that designated by the TEMP environment variable, or, failing that, in the root directory of your first hard-disk drive. These files have names beginning with ~WOA and are normally deleted when they are no longer needed.

To use the SWAPDISK variable, open your Windows SYSTEM.INI file (found in your main Windows directory) with a text editor, look for the section that begins with the line [NonWindowsApp], and add a line such as

```
swapdisk=d:\temp
```

Substitute the name of your drive and directory. Note that the directory must actually exist.

Disk space must exist for these temporary files. For this reason, you should always have at least 2MB of free space on the drive you have designated using SWAPDISK, the TEMP variable, or your root drive.

Virtual Memory in Enhanced Mode

In enhanced mode, all virtual memory is embodied in a single large disk file, which may be either a *temporary swap file,* which is created anew every time Windows starts, or a *permanent swap file,* which always occupies a fixed amount of space on a disk drive. The choice is left to you.

If you have enough disk space to spare (at least 2MB and preferably more), create a permanent swap file for maximum speed of access. Otherwise, you can allow Windows to create a temporary file at start-up. It will choose a drive and a size for the file on the basis of space available.

NOTE

Don't put a swap file on a drive handled by a disk-compression utility, such as Stacker or SuperStor.

Creating a Permanent Swap File

To set up a permanent swap file, follow these steps:

1. Identify the logical drive with the most space available.

2. Go through the drive's directories and delete any un-needed files.

3. Make the existing files on the drive contiguous using a disk defragmentation program, such as the Norton Utilities' SPEEDISK. The permanent swap file must be placed in contiguous free space, and the defragmentation program will make available the greatest possible amount of it. Note that the defragmentation program must be run from your original DOS prompt, not from Windows or from a copy of DOS started under Windows. Also, you should disable your disk cache before running the program.

4. Start Windows in enhanced mode and select, successively, the Control Panel, the 386 Enhanced Mode icon, the Virtual Memory command button, and the Change command button. Select your chosen drive, and select Permanent as the swap file type. You can accept the size for the file suggested (up to half the total free space on the drive) or type in a new size up to the maximum allowed.

5. Select OK until you are returned to the Control Panel. Restart Windows to put the changes into effect.

6. After creating the permanent swap file, you should not delete, rename, or move it. If you want to make any changes to its operation, make them through the Control Panel settings window that you just saw.

Speeding Disk Access

In enhanced mode, Windows is capable of reading from and writing to many disk drives directly in protected mode, in 32-bit chunks, a much faster means than the 16-bit access possible to DOS. The driver that provides this service is known as FastDisk.

Windows can use only a thoroughly standard, plain-vanilla disk controller (one compatible with the original AT controllers made by Western Digital) in this way. To see if Windows Setup qualified your controller, start Windows in enhanced mode and select the Control Panel, the 386 Enhanced Mode icon, the Virtual Memory command button, and the Change command button, just as you did to change a virtual-memory setting. See if a check box appears at the bottom of the window with the legend "Use 32-Bit Disk Access." To try FastDisk, check this box, click OK twice, and restart Windows.

Because some incompatibilities may exist undetected by Windows, you should try out some common operations, such as starting applications and printing, before using this feature in earnest. If Windows should hang on start-up with this setting, you can undo it by opening SYSTEM.INI for editing, locating the line "32BitDiskAccess=on," and editing it to read instead "32Bit-DiskAccess=off."

Virtual Memory on a Network

If you are running Windows on a network, there are a few further points to consider, especially to avoid long delays in operations:

✗ If you have a local hard disk with adequate free space, make sure that your swap file is created on it. In this case, virtual memory should work as well as on a stand-alone PC. (Otherwise, it will run very slowly.) To do this for standard mode, set the SWAPDISK variable in SYSTEM.INI to your local drive letter, using the steps described above. For enhanced mode and either a temporary swap file or a permanent one, choose the appropriate drive letter in the Virtual Memory dialog box.

✗ Enhanced mode cannot create a permanent swap file on a remote network drive (because of the low-level control it needs over this file). Rather, it will attempt to locate a suitable drive for a temporary file over the network connection every time it starts up. This can be a time-consuming process. You can save time by limiting the size of the swap file. Add this line to your SYSTEM.INI file under the heading [386Enh] (or edit the value, if the line already appears):

MaxPagingFileSize=1024

You can experiment with the value, but remember that it must equal at least 512 for virtual memory and paging to function at all, and that it must equal at least 1024 to do useful work.

Minimizing Use of Virtual Memory

The use of virtual memory is a last resort for Windows, because accessing the hard disk repeatedly is vastly slower than juggling applications in actual memory. You should make an effort to set up your system to minimize use of virtual memory by making more actual RAM available to Windows:

✗ If you have no more than 4MB of RAM in your PC, consider buying more RAM for your machine. It will pay for itself in improved productivity and stress reduction.

✗ Eliminate unneeded device drivers and TSRs so that less extended memory need be allocated as upper memory blocks.

✗ Make your disk cache and RAM disk no larger than needed (in line with the recommendations given earlier) to leave more extended memory free. If you are tempted to use a RAM disk created in XMS memory to hold swap files, note that you would avoid overhead by making the RAM disk proportionately smaller and leaving the memory free.

✗ Make sure that your memory manager is making all possible extended memory available as XMS memory. You will read more about how to determine this in coming chapters. In brief, you should avoid using QEMM's EXT-MEM= option to limit the amount of raw extended memory that QEMM handles. 386MAX users should avoid using its EXT= and EMS= options, which limit how much memory is made available as XMS. If you have more than 12MB of RAM, add this parameter to your DEVICE=QEMM386.SYS line:

EMBMEM=*nnnn*

where *nnnn* is how many kilobytes of RAM you have. This will maximize available memory by obliging QEMM to make all free memory available as XMS memory.

INSTALLING WINDOWS LAST

Things go smoothest when you install your memory manager after installing Windows. In this case, the memory manager setup program should locate Windows and make needed changes both to the memory manager configuration and to Windows system values. Similarly, when you update Windows and allow Windows Setup to overwrite your previous version, you probably need take no special action: Your previous settings will remain in place and valid. You may find yourself, however, making a new

Windows installation with QEMM or 386MAX up and running. In this case, you should check a few settings.

Settings in the Windows System File

These steps, which apply to Windows enhanced mode only, call for editing the SYSTEM.INI file in your Windows main directory. As always, use a text editor or a word processor in nondocument mode, and make a backup copy of the original file before making any changes.

Note that, in Windows system files, such as WIN.INI and SYS-TEM.INI, where some variables have only two possible values (these are called Boolean variables), the values True, Yes, On, and 1 are equivalent and interchangeable. Likewise, False, No, Off, and 0 all mean the same thing. Thus, if you see an instruction to change a variable to False and you find that its present value is 1, you can set it to 0, if you like, to maintain consistency.

For either QEMM or 386MAX, locate the section heading [386Enh] and add the following line below it (or see that it is already there and has the values shown):

SystemROMBreakPoint=false

This instruction will delegate the handling of certain system calls to the memory manager. If this value is set to True, Windows will assume a real memory address (near the top of DOS memory) is always available as a break point—an assumption that does not hold if Windows is started from V86 mode. If you are using QEMM, add this line:

VCPIWarning=false

It will eliminate warning messages in Windows about VCPI calls that QEMM will actually handle successfully.

You can let QEMM make these changes for you automatically, if you like, by running a utility supplied as part of the QEMM package. Just type

    qwinfix

at the DOS prompt and you are finished (this works only for versions 6.0 and later).

If you are using 386MAX, add this line in addition to System-ROMBreakPoint=false:

    VirtualHighDOS=-1

This instruction will enable a 386MAX feature that allows you to load different sets of device drivers and resident programs in different DOS windows.

If you are not using EMS, see the text describing settings for the ReservePageFrame=variable, earlier in this chapter.

Parameters to the Memory Manager

These changes belong in your CONFIG.SYS file at the end of the line invoking QEMM386.SYS or 386MAX.SYS. (In the case of 386MAX, alternatively, each can occur as a line by itself in the file 386MAX.PRO in your 386MAX directory.)

For either memory manager, you should remove the line

    DEVICE=C:\WINDOWS\HIMEM.SYS

which Windows Setup places at the top of CONFIG.SYS, because HIMEM.SYS will, at best, consume a few kilobytes of conventional memory and add overhead. The exception to this rule is if you are using QEMM with one of a very few Compaq or Compaq-clone EISA machines with more than 16MB of RAM.

For QEMM, in the case of enhanced mode only, the three parameters RAM, NOVIDEOFILL, and NOSORT should appear. For 386MAX, if the line EMS=0 appears in either CONFIG.SYS or 386MAX.PRO, you should remove it before installing Windows, or Windows Setup may hang. This parameter may also cause problems in standard mode and should be left out permanently if possible.

SETTING UP ALTERNATE CONFIGURATIONS

If you are one of those who spend time in and out of Windows, you may see the advantage of having alternate system configurations, one for running Windows and one for running DOS programs. For instance, the DOS configuration could take advantage of the memory manager's ability to sort memory or to extend the limits of conventional memory using QEMM's VIDRAM program (described in Chapter 5). It could load your favorite TSRs and use most of extended memory for a cache and a RAM disk. The Windows configuration could reserve plenty of space in conventional and extended memory for Windows and its applications. Once you have decided on your final configurations for Windows and your memory manager, you may want to refer back to this section.

NOTE

There are a number of freeware and shareware utilities that perform functions similar to what is described here. Check the CompuServe IBM Sys/Utilities Forum, Library, DOS Utilities section, to find several. (Try searching by the keyword config.)

You must first develop the two configurations, by having two pairs of CONFIG.SYS and AUTOEXEC.BAT files. First, make copies of your existing CONFIG.SYS and AUTOEXEC.BAT files, naming them, perhaps, CONFIG.OLD and AUTOEXEC.OLD. Set up CONFIG.SYS and AUTOEXEC.BAT optimally for your DOS applications, using (as always) a text editor or a word processor in nondocument mode. Use QEMM's OPTIMIZE program (described in Chapter 5) or Qualitas's MAXIMIZE program (described in Chapter 9) to make best use of high memory. Once this setup is working perfectly, copy CONFIG.SYS and AUTO-EXEC.BAT to two new files in the root directory of your boot drive. You might name them CONFIG.CMD and AUTOEXEC.CMD (as a mnemonic for the DOS *command* line).

Now, edit CONFIG.SYS and AUTOEXEC.BAT for Windows using the right parameters to the memory manager and removing unneeded resident programs. Run OPTIMIZE or MAXIMIZE and test the results by calling Windows (and then exiting). You could then optionally add the line

```
win
```

to the end of AUTOEXEC.BAT to call Windows automatically. Copy these two versions to new files called CONFIG.WIN and AUTOEXEC.WIN.

Create a batch file with these contents in a directory on your DOS PATH. Call the file, perhaps, RUNDOS.BAT:

```
@echo off
copy c:\config.cmd c:\config.sys >nul
copy c:\autoexec.cmd c:\autoexec.bat >nul
smartdrv /c
warmboot
```

The COPY commands will make your DOS command-line configuration files the current system files; the ending ">nul" will prevent COPY from writing to your screen and cluttering it with messages. The /c switch to SMARTDrive tells it to flush the cache, that is, to write all its contents to disk. This prevents immediately preceding operations (such as the COPY operations) from being lost when the system reboots. If you use a cache other than Windows SMARTDrive, substitute the command it uses for this action. Caches that don't delay disk writes (such as DOS 5's SMARTDrive) neither have nor need such an option. The WARMBOOT program reboots your computer. I'll show you how to create it in a moment.

Create a similar file called RUNWIN.BAT:

```
@echo off
copy c:\config.win c:\config.sys >nul
copy c:\autoexec.win c:\autoexec.bat >nul
smartdrv /c
warmboot
```

To create the WARMBOOT program, follow these steps precisely, like a cookbook:

1. Make the directory that holds RUNDOS.BAT and RUN-WIN.BAT current using the DOS CD command, as by entering

   ```
   cd c:\util
   ```

2. Create a file called WARMBOOT.SCR and enter this text *exactly*:

   ```
   N WARMBOOT.COM
   E 0100 B8 40 00 8E D8 C7 06 72
   ```

```
E 0108 00 34 12 EA 00 00 FF FF


RCX

10

W

Q
```

The text will tell DEBUG to enter 16 bytes of machine instructions at the proper location for a DOS COM program, write those 16 bytes to a file called WARMBOOT.COM, and quit. (A file recording a sequence of steps like this is called a *debug script*.)

3. Save the file, and give this command at the DOS prompt:

```
debug <warmboot.scr
```

Debug will read your script, follow the steps, and create the program.

Now, you can set up your system for DOS programs by simply entering RUNDOS at a DOS prompt, or for Windows programs by entering RUNWIN.

This chapter on memory issues with Windows winds up the overview of memory management using DOS and DOS applications. The rest of the book is devoted to the two major memory managers on the market: QEMM and 386MAX.

✗ PART II

GOING

BEYOND

THE LIMITS

WITH

QEMM

TWO ✗

Part II is devoted to QEMM. In Chapter 5, you will learn how to install
the program, how to work with the utilities included in the package,
and how to read and interpret QEMM's memory reports. Chapter 6
covers how to use the reporting program Manifest to help you diag-
nose problems with your system and applications. It also includes tips
on making QEMM work at its best with a number of popular programs
and common hardware environments. Look to Chapter 7, the QEMM
command reference, to learn how and when to use the various options
available with the memory manager and its companion programs.

CHAPTER FIVE

INTRODUCING

QEMM

Of the memory management packages available, QEMM from Quarterdeck goes the farthest to make every bit of DOS memory available to you, offering such services as Stealth to make upper address space do double duty. QEMM is very adaptable and reliable and includes the excellent reporting program, Manifest. This chapter will guide you through installing QEMM and using its basic tools.

The centerpiece of the QEMM package is the memory manager, QEMM386.SYS, which may be configured to supply extended and expanded memory, fill unused areas of upper memory and make them available to load device drivers and resident programs, and act as a VCPI or DPMI server. You will also find these supplemental tools:

✗ Programs (LOADHI.SYS and LOADHI.COM) actually to load devices or TSRs into upper memory, along with means to move your buffers and other DOS machinery there

✗ A program (VIDRAM.COM) for reclaiming unused video memory as conventional memory

✗ Programs for getting extra duty out of expanded memory

✗ A lean, command-line-driven program for controlling basic functions of the memory manager and for reporting on use of DOS memory (QEMM.COM)

✗ A rich menu-driven program for reporting on all aspects of your system (Manifest, or MFT.EXE)

✗ A program (OPTIMIZE.COM) to handle all the intricate work of fitting your system files and resident programs in upper memory

✗ Some small support files

✗ An installation program that loads files on your hard disk and orchestrates the task of conforming QEMM to your system configuration

INSTALLING QEMM

You should use the installation program to install QEMM; it expands the archived files from the distribution disk, brands your copy with registration information, and makes changes to your system files reflecting your requirements and system conformation. It also invokes OPTIMIZE to sort out how best to load your drivers and resident programs high. You may not have to make any changes to the setup INSTALL creates, but you should be prepared for the possibility, and that is what this chapter is about.

Here are a few tips:

✗ See that you have a half megabyte or so of free space on your boot drive.

✗ Have a bootable floppy disk on hand for the rare possibility that the installation process gets stuck. Try booting from it to make sure that it works.

✗ If you have any resident drivers or programs that normally load themselves into upper memory, edit CONFIG.SYS and AUTOEXEC.BAT and add options to prevent this— that is, to load them into conventional memory (to give QEMM the chance to load them into upper memory).

✗ If you can't prevent a driver or program from loading itself into upper memory, deactivate it for now by preceding the line that loads it with the word REM and a space. If you can't boot without the driver, however, let it be.

✗ If your AUTOEXEC.BAT file (or a batch file that it calls) ends by starting up an application, you may want to deactivate it for now by prefacing it with the word REM and a space. Doing this will expedite the optimizing process a little.

✗ Get used to seeing QEMM documentation call upper memory, high memory, and its contents high memory or high RAM. However, the term "High Memory Area" always refers to the first 64K of extended memory.

RUNNING INSTALL

It's time to get down to the business of installing QEMM. Note that the actual sequence and wording of screens may vary somewhat according to your present setup. Also note the screen messages. (Pressing the Escape key at some screens will take you back one screen; at others, it will exit you from the program.) Follow these steps:

1. Press Enter after reading the introductory screen and enter your registration information if prompted. Press Enter.

2. If you are installing DESQview 386, get to the screen for installing QEMM, by pressing Enter for a complete installation or by pressing P for a partial installation and then Q for QEMM.

3. Enter a drive and directory to hold the programs, or press Enter to accept the default directory.

4. A screen asks you if you would like to accept the default configuration (parameters to the line that loads QEMM386) or to change it. Press C to consider changing default values—this will introduce you to some common parameters, shown in Figure 5.1.

If you want to change any of these settings, press ↑ or ↓ to highlight it and select it by pressing the spacebar. INSTALL displays a window describing the parameter and showing possible values. You can make the change by typing in a legal value and pressing Enter. You can return to the configuration screen without making a change by pressing Esc.

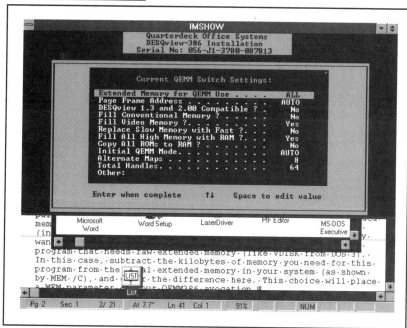

FIGURE 5.1: *Default QEMM settings*

Here is a summary of the settings:

Extended Memory for QEMM Use: You normally want the ALL parameter to allow QEMM to take over your entire pool of extended memory and make it available to applications (including Windows) that use EMS or XMS or available to VCPI or DPMI clients. You would only want to reduce this amount if you use some primitive driver or program that needs raw extended memory (like VDISK from DOS 3). In this case, subtract the kilobytes of memory you need for this program from the total extended memory in your system (as shown by MEM /C), and enter the difference here. This choice will add the MEM parameter to your QEMM386 line.

Page Frame Address: The value of AUTO allows QEMM to search out a 64K block of upper memory (or conventional memory, if necessary) to place the EMS page frame. If you know where you want the page frame, you can edit this value to a chosen position, adding the FRAME=*nnnn* (or FR=*nnnn*) value to QEMM386. After you've read the troubleshooting tips in the next chapter, you may find reason to do this.

DESQview 1.3 and 2.00 Compatible?: This setting should be left to No unless you are actually using DESQview version 2.00 or earlier. The value of Yes will add the OLDDV parameter to QEMM386, causing it to occupy a few more kilobytes of conventional memory.

Fill Conventional Memory?: You can set this to Yes if you have less than 640K of conventional memory in your PC; this will instruct QEMM386 to map EMS 4.0 memory into your conventional memory range. Note, however, that this action is incompatible with Windows enhanced mode. If you have less than 640K and leave this set to No, the NOFILL (or NO) parameter will be added to the QEMM386 line.

Fill Video Memory?: The default setting, Yes, will allow QEMM to find unused areas of address space assigned to video cards and fill them with RAM to assign as upper memory blocks. The position and extent of these areas depend on what type of video adapter you have. If you use Windows enhanced mode, you should edit this setting to No, because the Yes setting interferes with Windows' operation. Then, the parameter NOVIDEOFILL (or NV) will be added to the QEMM386 line.

Replace Slow Memory with Fast?: This setting controls whether QEMM will test all your RAM for speed and map the fastest RAM into conventional memory. You can easily use Manifest later to determine if this function would be helpful. At any rate, it is incompatible with Windows en-hanced mode. Leaving the value No adds the parameter NOSORT (or NS) to the QEMM386 line.

Fill All High Memory with RAM?: If this is set to Yes, RAM is mapped from extended memory into all available upper memory blocks (excluding addresses occupied by ROM or adapter RAM or by the page frame). The RAM parameter is added to the QEMM386 line; it is essential to loading your programs high and necessary to Windows operation (unless you have set certain other parameters).

Copy All ROMs to RAM?: If this is set to Yes, the ROM parameter is added to the QEMM386 line and QEMM takes care of providing shadow RAM—RAM that effectively replaces much slower ROM in your system. If your PC BIOS already provides shadow RAM, the RAM parameter is redundant. You can easily learn if your PC has built-in shadow RAM (and if QEMM recognizes it) by using Manifest, as described in the next chapter.

TIP

Some ROM code has built-in timing dependencies, that is, assump-tions about how fast the code will execute. (This is not a good programming practice.) You will sometimes find this in ROMs for disk or tape drives: The code will initiate some drive operation at in-struction x and assume that the operation is complete by instruction y. If the code is sped up, the operation will fail. If you see cases like this, you will have to identify and remove the ROM= parameter for the offending ROM.

Initial QEMM Mode: There are three possible values for this setting—ON, OFF, and AUTO—which control whether QEMM always puts the system into virtual 86 mode, never does so, or does so as required to provide EMS, XMS, and related services. The default value, AUTO, is appropriate for everything but special operations, such as analyzing DOS memory. Some other parameters, such as RAM, ROM, and values that provide sorting or filling, result in QEMM running in V86 mode anyway.

Alternate Maps: This setting allocates data areas out of extended memory to hold current CPU register values for each running program in a multitasking environment, like DESQview. You can set this value to the maximum number of programs that you expect to run at once under DESQview, plus 1. The default value is 8. Note that Windows does not use this value, so if you don't use DESQview, you can probably reduce this setting to 0, which adds the parameter MAPS=0 to the QEMM386 line. Each map takes up about 4K of extended memory.

Total Handles: These are numerical values given serially to each program using EMS or XMS memory, so the value here limits the number of EMS users that can run at once. You can set a value anywhere between 16 and 255; the default is 64. Note that QEMM itself takes one handle to make it possible to map conventional memory. The parameter added to the QEMM386 line is HANDLES=*nn* (HA=*nn*).

Other: You can add other parameters here that you *know* are needed for QEMM386. As a rule, you should avoid adding extra parameters unless you understand them thoroughly, both because their meanings may not be obvious and because INSTALL generally does a good job of determining needed parameters. The chapters in this part will help you to understand what QEMM386 parameters do.

Once you are happy with the settings on the Current QEMM Switch Settings screen, press Enter and continue with the installation:

1. Press Enter to allow INSTALL to make proposed changes to your CONFIG.SYS and AUTOEXEC.BAT files (adding the line invoking QEMM.SYS and putting the QEMM

directory on the path), or press N if you wish to make the changes yourself later. If you have a line loading a memory manager already, INSTALL will next ask permission to remove it—you can press Enter to give your blessing. Watch the program expand files and copy them to the new directory.

2. INSTALL will look for a copy of Windows. If it finds one, it will ask you to confirm that it has found your usual path to Windows; if not, it will ask you if you use Windows and ask you to provide a path. At this point, it will ask permission to make certain settings in your Windows SYSTEM.INI file (to make the settings SystemROMBreakPoint=false and VCPIWarning=false). You can allow INSTALL to make the changes, or you can make them later by running QWINFIX (just enter QWINFIX from the DOS command prompt, and you are finished).

3. Press Enter to read the help file READQ.ME (or press N to skip it). You should peruse this material to look for notes on your hardware and software. You can navigate it by pressing PgUp and PgDn; press Enter when you are finished.

4. Basic installation is complete. You can remove the distribution disk and press Enter to run OPTIMIZE, or you can press Esc to return to DOS. Running OPTIMIZE is a very good idea.

Running OPTIMIZE

OPTIMIZE is a separate program from INSTALL that manipulates the contents of your CONFIG.SYS and AUTOEXEC.BAT files (as well as batch files called from AUTOEXEC.BAT using the CALL command) to make best use of upper memory to hold your devices and resident programs. OPTIMIZE may also load your DOS buffers high if you are not using DOS 5 or if you are not using the DOS=HIGH line. (See more details on buffers later in this chapter.)

OPTIMIZE uses LOADHI.SYS and LOADHI.COM with special options to determine how much memory programs need to initialize and run and so where to place them. Basically, OPTIMIZE performs what has been a classic job for computers since computers have existed: a repetitious task that you or I might find unbearably tedious, in this case juggling all possible permutations of loading orders for drivers and programs and picking the most space-efficient one. The whole process usually takes just a couple of minutes.

You should run OPTIMIZE, not only on initial installation, but whenever you add, remove, or reconfigure hardware devices, software device-drivers, or resident programs, because all these can change patterns of upper memory use. OPTIMIZE runs in three phases:

1. The setup phase, in which it creates backup copies of your existing CONFIG.SYS and AUTOEXEC.BAT files (or as modified by INSTALL), which it calls CONFIG.QDK and AUTOEXEC.QDK.

2. The detection phase, in which it detects and loads your drivers and resident programs and finds how much memory each needs to initialize and run. It then determines which programs can be loaded into upper memory and presents an analysis of its results.

3. The final phase, in which it attempts to load those programs into upper memory and makes final changes to your system files if successful.

The transition between each phase is marked by a reboot of your machine. For your part, you just follow these steps to use OPTIMIZE:

1. If you are starting from the DOS command prompt (not running INSTALL), make your QEMM path the current drive and directory (by entering **c:** and then **cd \qemm**), and then enter **optimize**.

2. Read the opening screen and press Enter.

3. Read the notes on the setup phase and press Enter. (There is another choice here: You can press O to force OPTIMIZE to test Stealth techniques or to do further analysis of your system. These options are normally taken only after a standard optimization leads to problems; they are discussed later in this chapter.)

4. Read the note on the detection phase, press Enter, and observe the reboot.

5. Read the Analysis screen. The opening sentence tells you how many "high RAM regions" (separate contiguous blocks of upper memory) were found and how many total drivers and resident programs were found to load into them. The table will look something like Figure 5.2.

   It tells you the following:

   ✗ How many programs OPTIMIZE succeeded in loading into upper memory

   ✗ How much conventional memory was consumed by those that wouldn't fit into upper memory

   ✗ How much upper memory was consumed by those that would fit

   ✗ The biggest chunk of upper memory that was left over

   ✗ How much upper memory was left over in total

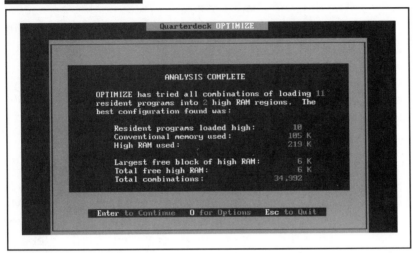

FIGURE 5.2: *The Analysis output*

✗ How many ways of arranging devices and resident programs OPTIMIZE tried

If you see room for improvement in these figures, you should finish this first run of OPTIMIZE and then try some of the steps described below.

6. Press Enter here to continue with the basic setup and bypass the fancy stuff described next. If you press O, you can study several advanced displays of what OPTIMIZE is doing. In the latter case, you are given a choice of three ways to assess or control the optimization:

✗ Choose Display the Region Layout to see a table of the memory block numbers and addresses that the programs will occupy, or (by then pressing F1) a table of sizes and addresses of the upper memory blocks themselves.

✗ Choose Modify the Data Collected... to see a screen (Figure 5.3) showing the initial and final sizes of

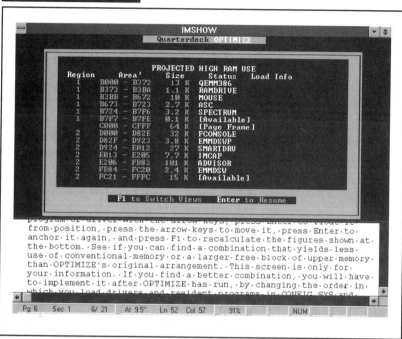

FIGURE 5.3: *Data for the OPTIMIZE process*

programs, whether OPTIMIZE is attempting to load them high, and if and how it is providing extra space for them to initialize themselves (whether by temporarily loading them into the page frame or into another unspecified memory space). You should not attempt to change these values; the ability to edit them has been placed here for highly specialized purposes.

✗ Choose to play "what-if" to see the effects of changing the load order of drivers and TSRs. To try this, use the arrow keys to select a resident program or driver, press Enter to detach it from its current position, press the arrow keys to move it, press Enter to anchor it again, and press F1 to recalculate the figures shown at the bottom. See if you can find a combination that yields less use of conventional memory or a larger free block of upper memory than OPTIMIZE's original arrangement. This screen is only for your information. If you find a better combination, you will have to implement it after OPTIMIZE has run, by changing the order in which you load drivers and resident programs in CONFIG.SYS and AUTOEXEC.BAT. You should then run OPTIMIZE again. Note that some drivers and resident programs must be loaded in a particular order to function. For now, you can return to the Analysis screen by pressing Esc.

7. At this point, INSTALL may display a screen suggesting that Stealth should be incorporated into your setup. This only happens if there is not enough room to load all your programs into upper memory. Stealth, which is a system for reclaiming address space devoted to ROM as upper memory, is invoked only if necessary, because it slows down your computer a bit and may lead to conflicts in use of upper memory or interrupt handling. You can press Enter to allow INSTALL to check your PC for Stealth compatibility, or press Esc to bypass this step and do without Stealth. If you press Enter, follow these steps (otherwise, go to step 8):

✗ Read a screen describing the testing process and press Enter. Note that you will need a floppy disk to allow INSTALL to test the disk-drive BIOS. You can use any formatted floppy that your A drive can read.

✗ Press Enter to let INSTALL try out the Stealth:M system. Stealth:M is the most efficient form of Stealth, but the alternative, Stealth:F, may be more widely compatible, so it makes sense to try Stealth:M first.

✗ The Stealth testing phase begins. Press Enter to allow a reboot of your PC. Note the "Video test in progress" phrase that appears on your screen several times. Insert the floppy disk, remove it, and press a key as prompted.

✗ Press Enter to accept the Stealth:M parameter, if it was successful. Otherwise, select Stealth:F and follow the same sequence of steps you followed for Stealth:M.

8. Read the final-phase screen and press Enter. The PC will reboot. You should watch the screen like a hawk for any error messages as CONFIG.SYS and AUTOEXEC.BAT are executed. Watch especially for "Not enough room to load *programname* high, loading low" messages, which indicate that OPTIMIZE did not successfully guess the program's memory requirements.

9. Press Enter at the completion screen to return to the DOS prompt.

What If Something Hangs?

Occasionally, something may cause the optimization process to stop cold. The problem is usually a driver or resident program, or a conflict arising when QEMM maps RAM over unrecognized device ROM or RAM in upper memory. To resolve the problem, try the steps below one at a time. If you can't get back to a DOS prompt or reboot normally, boot from your floppy system-disk and restore your setup as modified by INSTALL by entering **c:\qemm\unopt** at the DOS prompt. This command runs a small batch file that copies CONFIG.QDK to CONFIG.SYS and AUTO-EXEC.QDK to AUTOEXEC.BAT.

You can then try some of the modifications to your system files described below. Note that the case of letters in QEMM parameters does not matter; parameters are shown in uppercase below to be consistent with how INSTALL and OPTIMIZE handle case.

TIP 》》

You can view QEMM386 messages before they scroll away by adding the PAUSE parameter to the command line. Similarly, view LOADHI.SYS or LOADHI.COM output by adding the /PAUSE parameter before the name of the command being loaded.

1. Make sure that your CONFIG.SYS and AUTOEXEC.BAT files are correctly formatted. In particular, make sure that AUTOEXEC.BAT is not over 512 lines long, and make sure that no single line is over about 100 characters in length. OPTIMIZE cannot read lines over 128 characters long, and it lengthens some lines in the course of optimization. If you use a command interpreter other than COMMAND.COM, prevent OPTIMIZE from trying to load internal commands (like DIR or COPY in COMMAND.COM) high: Create a text file called OPTIMIZE.EXC (meaning "exclude from optimization") in your QEMM directory, and place such commands in the file, one command per line.

NOTE 》》

A command interpreter is the program that supplies the DOS prompt and interprets your commands by taking some action (like displaying a directory of files) if what you type matches an internal table of commands, or by searching the path for a program to load otherwise. It also handles functions like redirecting input and output, and interpreting batch files. There are a number of third-party replacements for COMMAND.COM. Some, for instance, emulate the UNIX Bourne or C shell.

2. If you are using Stealth, try reoptimizing without it: Remove the ST:M or ST:F parameter from the QEMM386.SYS line in your CONFIG.SYS file and then run OPTIMIZE, bypassing the Stealth check. If your system now runs, see the troubleshooting notes on Stealth in the next chapter.

3. Try adding the parameters NOSH and NT (for "don't try
to reclaim shadow RAM" and "don't use top memory") to
the QEMM386 line in CONFIG.SYS, and run OPTIMIZE
again. (Many 386 and 486 PCs have ROM shadowing (substituting fast RAM for ROM BIOS) built into their hardware. OPTIMIZE attempts to detect the kind of ROM
shadowing in use (usually one of five kinds supplied by
Chip and Technologies) and reclaim surplus RAM. If it
misidentifies the form of ROM shadowing, it can cause
trouble.

✗ If these parameters do not allow OPTIMIZE to run
successfully, remove them and go to step 4.

✗ If you can now run OPTIMIZE, try removing the NT
parameter. If you are still successful, your problem
was with ROM shadowing. Reboot your PC and
bring up its setup program by pressing a key given in
a message after the memory check (often DEL). If you
can turn off hardware ROM shadowing, do so and
then add the ROM parameter to the QEMM386 line to
have QEMM take over the job. Otherwise, leave
NOSH in place.

✗ If NT solves your problems, try removing NOSH.
Some PCs place 384K of memory just below the 16MB
mark (where it is called "top memory"), and your PC
may be managing it in a way incompatible with
QEMM. The NT parameter tells QEMM to leave this
area alone.

4. Find out if your PC has a bus-mastering controller (probably
a SCSI controller) for disk drives or other devices. If so, try
adding the parameter DB=10 to the QEMM386 line. If this
works, try to obtain a VDS driver from the controller

manufacturer and install it according to the instructions provided, instead of using the parameter. The driver may solve other problems, such as might occur with Windows enhanced mode.

NOTE ⟫

VDS stands for Virtual DMA Services. The driver is designed to mediate between direct memory access by the controller and memory remapping by a memory manager, as described in Chapter 4.

5. Run OPTIMIZE again, and press O (for Options) from the Setup screen.

6. Press Enter to have OPTIMIZE search for memory that should be excluded (not mapped by QEMM). Follow the prompts, which include messages to turn off your PC and turn it back on after 10 seconds. If OPTIMIZE proposes further exclusions, press Enter to accept them. (You can see where the exclusions fall at this point by pressing F1, but do not attempt to edit them.) The optimization process goes on as usual from this point. If it succeeds, leave the resulting X= parameter on the QEMM386 line.

7. Try adding the NOROMHOLES (NRH) parameter to the QEMM386 line to prevent QEMM from filling small areas of ROM (which may be occupied by unidentified device memory). Then, follow the analysis procedures described in Chapter 6 to precisely identify upper memory that should be excluded.

8. Create a simple configuration by deactivating your drivers and resident programs:

✗ Add the word REM and a space before the command that loads each one (excepting QEMM).

✗ Remove the word REM from a single driver and run OPTIMIZE again.

✗ Continue this process until it fails.

✗ Create a file called OPTIMIZE.EXC in your QEMM directory (if you haven't already), and add the command name of the offending program to the file on a line by itself. This will allow the program to load in conventional memory as before. Some programs won't operate in upper memory, or won't even work with LOADHI as it attempts to learn their memory needs (using the /GS parameter).

Refer to Chapter 6 for some tricks for making room for programs that load themselves high.

What If There's Not Enough Room?

OPTIMIZE may report that it is unable to load all your programs high. Sometimes, too, a program may fail to load high when OPTIMIZE underestimates the space that it needs. In either case, you may be able to make more space available in upper memory.

How can you judge the program's success in loading programs into upper memory? One simple test is to enter

loadhi

with no parameters at a command prompt. LOADHI will give you a report like the one shown in Figure 5.4.

It shows you the regions and precise areas in upper memory that are occupied or free, as well as the occupant of each occupied space. You can assume that programs that do not appear here have been loaded in conventional memory. The hex numbers represent addresses beyond the 640K mark. You can translate them into decimal equivalents using the rules in Appendix A, if you find this helpful.

Region	Area	Size	Status
1	B000 - B2B7	10K	Used (MOUSE)
1	B2B8 - B3AC	3.8K	Used (EMMDSWP)
1	B3AD - B3C6	0.4K	Used (UMB)
1	B3C7 - B44D	2.1K	Used (EMMDSW)
1	B44E - B4FE	2.7K	Available
2	CC00 - CC04	0.1K	Used (UMB)
2	CC05 - D2EE	27K	Used (SMARTDRV)
2	D2EF - D2FE	0.2K	Available
3	F600 - F647	1.1K	Used (RAMDRIVE)
3	F648 - F6FF	2.8K	Used (UMB)

FIGURE 5.4: *A LOADHI report*

Another simple test provides an introduction to Manifest. Enter **mft** at the DOS prompt, press F (for First Meg), and press R (for Programs). The programs that you see above the legend "Conventional memory ends at 640K" are in conventional memory; those below it are in upper memory. You may be able to see more programs by pressing PgDn, as indicated. You can exit Manifest by pressing Esc twice.

Here are some ideas for making more upper memory available for filling with RAM:

✗ If any programs failed to load high at the conclusion of the optimization process, and OPTIMIZE did not invoke Stealth, run OPTIMIZE again but force it to try Stealth by choosing the Stealth test as an option from the Setup Phase notification screen.

✗ Analyze your system to find areas that QEMM has excluded from availability and that you can actually include. This topic is covered in Chapter 6.

✗ Position your hardware drivers' BIOS areas in a way that consolidates free memory, or at address spaces that leave the largest possible blocks of contiguous free memory behind. You will easily be able to learn where to relocate a ROM block after studying the Manifest QEMM-386 Type screens described in Chapter 6. The ability actually to relocate the BIOS must be built into the hardware itself.

✗ Remove the EMS page frame using the FRAME=NONE parameter to QEMM386; this gains 64K of free memory. This will not be possible if any of your applications use expanded memory, if you are using Stealth, or if LOADHI is using the frame to give programs space to initialize (that is, if any LOADHI line uses the /SQF parameter). Because so many programs may use the page frame, you should approach this option with great caution.

You may be able to make more conventional memory available by using the VIDRAM program described later.

USING THE QEMM CONTROL PROGRAM

QEMM.COM is a simple program that runs from the DOS command line. You can think of it as two programs in one: The first controls basic memory manager functions, and the second reports on DOS memory usage. In this latter capacity, it duplicates some of the functions available in Manifest, the more elaborate, menu-driven reporting program.

You use QEMM by typing it as a DOS command, giving it one or more options (called switches or parameters). For instance, try entering

    qemm ?

to see a list of QEMM options, or

    qemm help

to see all options accompanied by brief descriptions. Many options have shorter forms to save you typing; they appear in parentheses after the longer form. (For instance, you can type **me** or **mem** for *memory*.)

You can enter **qemm summary** (or **qemm sum**) to see a short report on the current QEMM operating mode (ON or OFF), to see how much expanded memory is available (and if expanded memory is being used), and to see where the EMS page frame is located.

Using QEMM to Control Memory Management

QEMM.COM has three options to control the operation of QEMM386.SYS:

✗ Enter **qemm on** to place QEMM in V86 mode.

✗ Enter **qemm off** to place QEMM in real mode.

✗ Enter **qemm auto** to allow QEMM to switch in and out of V86 mode as an application demands expanded memory.

You may find little or no everyday use for any of these commands. In particular, if you have set QEMM to fill memory, map RAM or ROM in upper memory, sort conventional memory, or provide expanded memory, QEMM cannot be turned off.

Two additional options may occasionally be helpful when you have placed the QEMM command in a batch file. If you place

qemm nope %1

as a line in a batch file, you can give an argument to the batch file (such as *on*), and you will not be prompted to unload QEMM from memory when the line is executed. On the contrary, if you enter the line

qemm pause

you will be prompted to press Esc to cease using the memory manager, when the line is executed.

Using QEMM Report Functions

QEMM's report functions are basic to knowing and analyzing how your system memory is allocated and how your DOS memory is classified and used. They offer the big picture of how your RAM is being assigned as well as two kinds of views of DOS memory that will appear again and again as you work out optimal use of conventional and upper memory. Thus, it's worth taking a few minutes to understand how these functions work.

Memory: The Big Picture

Enter **qemm memory** (or **mem** or **me**) to see a kind of balance sheet for QEMM, similar to that shown in Figure 5.5.

You can also view this screen in fancier dress as Manifest's QEMM-386 Memory screen, reached by pressing Q and M.

Extended This is raw extended memory (as opposed to XMS memory); the "Initial" figure is all of your system RAM minus blocks that your PC has dedicated to other purposes (conventional memory, shadow RAM, or top memory), which are placed on lines of their own. If you have loaded other drivers or memory

```
                     Unavailable  Converted
              Initial  to QEMM    by QEMM    Leaving
Conventional:   640K  -    0K  -      0K  =   640K
Extended:      7168K  -    0K  -   7168K  =     0K
Shadow RAM:     384K  -  208K  -    176K  =     0K
Expanded:         0K  -    0K  +   7056K  =  7056K
High RAM:         0K  -    0K  +    116K  =   116K
              ------    ------    ------    ------
   TOTAL:      8192K  -  208K  -    172K  =  7812K

              172K QEMM Overhead
   Code & Data:    79K     Maps:          32K
   Tasks:          18K     Mapped ROM:    20K
   DMA Buffer:     12K     Unassigned:    11K
          3K Conventional Memory Overhead
```

FIGURE 5.5: *A QEMM memory report*

managers before QEMM, they may have made some memory "unavailable to QEMM." (Note that it is generally not a good idea to do this; it's better to load such drivers later, leaving them raw memory through the EXTMEM parameter if necessary.)

QEMM will convert all this memory and make it available under EMS, XMS, VCPI, or DPMI unless you limit the amount using one of two parameters having opposite effects: EXTMEM (or EXT) specifies a number in kilobytes that QEMM should leave alone. MEMORY (or MEM or ME) specifies a number of kilobytes that QEMM should manage. The EXT value (or the initial value minus the ME value) will appear in the "Leaving" column. This amount of memory is left at the bottom end of extended memory for programs that need raw extended memory (such as DOS's former VDISK program). This amount will go to waste as far as Windows, Paradox, and other XMS or expanded memory clients are concerned.

Conventional   Initial conventional memory is the RAM that your PC devotes to conventional memory. If this amount is 1K or 2K short of 640K, this fact is a tip-off that your machine has an extended BIOS data area (XBDA). This area can be a source of problems if a program assumes that the XBDA is at this location, after QEMM has relocated it. You can solve the problem by placing the NX parameter on the QEMM386 line.

If you have a monochrome or CGA video adapter, QEMM should have converted RAM to bring total conventional memory to 704K or 736K, respectively. Conversely, if QEMM was obliged to place the page frame in conventional memory (probably because 64K of contiguous upper memory was not available), it should have subtracted 64K from the total. Finally, if QEMM has backfilled your memory to 640K (supplied the missing memory by remapping it from extended memory, if your motherboard has less than 640K), that should appear as a positive conversion value.

Shadow RAM   The figure under Shadow RAM should meet your expectations of the amount of shadow RAM created by the BIOS (the initial value), the amount actually dedicated to shadowing ROMs (unavailable), and the surplus that QEMM was able to appropriate (converted).

Top Memory   Some PCs (including some made by Compaq and Micronics) appropriate the top 384K of the 16MB address space (16000K to 16384K) for ROM shadowing. If this is true of your PC, a line similar to the Shadow RAM line but labeled Top Memory should appear here. If you see a line for top memory when your PC has none, or if you have other problems with top memory, try adding the NT parameter to the QEMM386 line.

Expanded   Initial expanded memory is dedicated memory on an EMS board. Converted expanded memory is what QEMM creates out of raw extended memory; it is also (with certain exceptions—see the entry for the EMBMEM parameter in Chapter 7) approximately the amount of memory QEMM will make available as XMS or protected-mode memory.

High RAM   Converted high RAM refers to upper memory blocks created by QEMM out of raw extended memory.

The lower section of the screen shows memory QEMM takes to do its job.

QEMM Overhead   The QEMM overhead is in extended memory. The following are subcategories of QEMM overhead:

Code & Data: The QEMM386 memory manager itself.

Tasks: Data structures allocated to transferring data used to handle interrupts from protected mode, in which QEMM normally operates, to real mode, in which DOS must finally attend to the interrupts. The 18K of memory reflects the default 16 tasks, a number that can be raised using the TASKS= (TA=) parameter to QEMM386.

DMA Buffer: An area of memory used to translate the real memory addresses that devices like disk or tape drives or network cards use for direct memory access (which bypasses the CPU) to the mapped memory addresses created by QEMM. If a device such as a tape drive fails (with or without an error message saying that the DMA area is too small), you can increase the size of the buffer using the DMA= (DM=) parameter to QEMM386, which you can follow with a number from 12 to 128, representing kilobytes.

Maps: DESQview uses maps to store CPU register values used by different processes (programs in action). The 32K size reflects the default value of eight maps. You can give QEMM386 a new MAPS= (or MA=) parameter setting of up to 56K if you run more than seven programs concurrently; your system will run more efficiently. On the other hand, if you don't use DESQview, you can save extended memory by setting the parameter MAPS=0.

Mapped ROM: Extended memory that QEMM appropriates to replace ROM in the address space of your machine. You use it (by adding the ROM parameter to the QEMM386 line) when you don't have built-in ROM shadowing or when you have certain ROMs that ROM shadowing doesn't cover. QEMM also automatically maps the 4K area of the ROM BIOS used to reboot your PC (starting at F800), allowing it to monitor the reboot process. It maps other ROMs on certain PCs.

Unassigned: Odd scraps of leftover memory.

Conventional Memory Overhead   Conventional

memory overhead is the small part of QEMM386 that must be placed in conventional memory.

DOS Memory Types

Enter **qemm type** (or **qemm t**) at the DOS prompt to see how DOS memory is broken into sections (see Figure 5.6).

The area from 0000 to 9FFF is conventional memory; QEMM will leave the first 64K alone, but the rest is, in principle, mappable (available for an EMS page frame or backfilling).

Note that, in hexadecimal numbering, 9FFF is one less than A000, just as, in decimal numbering, 9999 is one less than 10,000. This is why, when you specify areas of memory to QEMM (as you will when you include or exclude them), you should specify an ending address whose last two digits are FF. If instead, for instance, you specify a range A000-C000, QEMM will include the 4K of memory beginning at C000. If you are using Stealth, it will act on the 16K beginning at C000 (because Stealth uses expanded memory, which can't be allocated in smaller units). Specify A000-BFFF instead.

```
          Area          Size         Status
      0000  -  0FFF      64K      Excluded
      1000  -  9FFF     576K      Mappable
      A000  -  AFFF      64K      Video
      B000  -  B7FF      32K      High RAM
      B800  -  BFFF      32K      Video
      C000  -  C7FF      32K      ROM
      C800  -  CBFF      16K      Mapped ROM
      CC00  -  DFFF      80K      High RAM
      E000  -  EFFF      64K      Page Frame
      F000  -  F5FF      24K      ROM
      F600  -  F6FF       4K      High RAM
      F700  -  F7FF       4K      ROM
      F800  -  F8FF       4K      Mapped ROM
      F900  -  FFFF      28K      ROM
```

FIGURE 5.6: *An example of DOS memory types*

Upper memory extends from A000 to FFFF. The TYPE display shows you a complete breakdown of this area.

QEMM's LIST (or L) parameter is synonymous with TYPE. If you enter **qemm** alone on the command line, you will get a combined display of SUMMARY and TYPE.

The QEMM ACCESSED and ANALYSIS parameters also display memory in this general format; you use them when seeking additional memory to include or exclude. Together with the RESET parameter, they are described in Chapter 6.

DOS Memory Maps

You can get another view of DOS memory by entering **qemm type map**, or simply **qemm map** (see Figure 5.7).

Some areas will be highlighted or colored on your display. Each square in the grid represents 4K of memory, the smallest area that QEMM can fill. Each square has a beginning address with zeros in the ones and tens places, but, as you go across a row from left to right, the digit in the hundreds place increases from 0 to F in steps. Adding the hexadecimal value 100 to a segment address in a step like this represents a 4K jump in memory.

```
        n=0123 4567 89AB CDEF
0n00 XXXX XXXX XXXX XXXX
1n00 ++++ ++++ ++++ ++++
2n00 ++++ ++++ ++++ ++++        + = Mappable
3n00 ++++ ++++ ++++ ++++        * = Rammable
4n00 ++++ ++++ ++++ ++++        F = Page Frame
5n00 ++++ ++++ ++++ ++++        H = High RAM
6n00 ++++ ++++ ++++ ++++        M = Mapped ROM
7n00 ++++ ++++ ++++ ++++        X = Excluded
8n00 ++++ ++++ ++++ ++++        V = Video
9n00 ++++ ++++ ++++ ++++        A = Adapter RAM
An00 VVVV VVVV VVVV VVVV        R = ROM
Bn00 HHHH HHHH VVVV VVVV        / = Split ROM
Cn00 RRRR RRRR MMMM HHHH
Dn00 HHHH HHHH HHHH HHHH
En00 FFFF FFFF FFFF FFFF
Fn00 RRRR RRHR MRRR RRRR
```

FIGURE 5.7: *An example of a DOS memory map*

Columns are in groups of four, so each group represents 16K; that is, adding 400 to a segment address means a 16K jump in memory. Each group of four begins with a digit in the hundreds place of 0, 4, 8, or C. When you enter a segment address like this (for instance, E000, E400, E800, or EC00), you specify a memory address at a 16K boundary. A page frame must begin at a 16K boundary, so it must start at a segment address like this.

A whole row of 16 squares represents 64K of memory, so each row begins at a 64K boundary; that is, each row begins at a segment address formed by a digit followed by three zeros: When you add 1000 to a segment address, you add 64K to the memory location you are pointing to. Thus, the segment address A000 points exactly to the 640K mark, the beginning of upper memory.

To see the beginning address for a block of memory, replace the *n* value in its first row with the *n*= digit in its first column. To see the ending address, find the beginning address for the last square and add FF. For instance, look at the mapped ROM (marked by M's) in the Cn00 row. It begins in the 8 column, so the beginning address is C800. It ends in the B column, so the whole address range is C800-CBFF (as the QEMM TYPE output above confirms). Refer to the legend on the right to see how types of memory are marked.

- ✗ Mappable memory can be remapped. Rammable memory is available to be filled with RAM but cannot be remapped (because it is under the EMS 16K size minimum).

- ✗ The "Page Frame," naturally, shows the current location of the EMS page frame.

- ✗ High RAM represents areas of upper memory that QEMM has filled with RAM and so has made available for loading device drivers and resident programs.

- ✗ Mapped ROM is ROM that QEMM itself has replaced with RAM for faster operation.

- ✗ Excluded memory comprises areas that QEMM has been prohibited from remapping or filling, usually by the EXCLUDE= (or X=) parameter on the QEMM386 line.

- ✗ Video memory is RAM or ROM used by your video adapter. Here, the A000 line is occupied by VGA graphics RAM; the B000 line holds text RAM followed by video ROM.

- ✗ Adapter RAM is memory excluded by use of the ADAP-TERRAM= (or ARAM=) parameter rather than the EX-CLUDE= parameter. You may use ARAM= simply to document for yourself what an area of memory is doing.

- ✗ ROM is actual ROM or Shadow RAM.

- ✗ Split ROM shows that ROM is occupying less than a full 4K cell. An area like this is too small for QEMM to replace with RAM using the ROM parameter.

You can see screens in this format by entering **qemm accessed map** or **qemm analysis map**—these commands are covered in the next chapter. Manifest also provides several screens in this format.

FREEING CONVENTIONAL MEMORY WITH LOADHI

QEMM uses two small programs to place drivers and resident programs in upper memory: LOADHI.SYS for drivers and LOAD-HI.COM for resident programs. In practically every case, your best choice in using them is to run OPTIMIZE as described previously and allow OPTIMIZE to add, subtract, or modify LOADHI commands with the appropriate arguments. You can then enter **load-hi** by itself on the DOS command line to see a report on where your programs have been loaded and how much space they are occupying.

If you want to experiment with LOADHI.COM, note that the command syntax is

    loadhi [*parameters to loadhi*] yourcommand [*any parameters to yourcommand*]

LOADHI.SYS works the same way, except that it always appears in CONFIG.SYS preceded by DEVICE= without a space.

For instance, you can see for yourself how much space a program will require as it is initialized and once it is loaded by using LOADHI's /GS (for "get size") parameter. To try this with a small TSR called FOO.COM, you enter

    loadhi /gs foo

You receive the report

LOADHI: 2096 run-time bytes (3K)

LOADHI: 2928 resident bytes (3K)

LOADHI: This program MAY use SQUEEZEF

The program will require about 3K of free upper memory to run.

 NOTE

You can read more about LOADHI parameters in the QEMM command reference in Chapter 7.

FREEING CONVENTIONAL MEMORY WITH THE DOS RESOURCE PROGRAMS

QEMM's DOS resource programs are replacements for DOS resources (buffers, file handles, file control blocks, and the LASTDRIVE variable). The advantage of the QEMM versions is that they can be loaded into upper memory using LOADHI. The OPTIMIZE program will load buffers high if this action is appropriate to your system. The other resources consume much less memory, but you may find it worthwhile to load them high manually.

Buffers

Your DOS buffers make up a kind of primitive disk cache (which is still much better than none). When you first read data from a disk, DOS puts the data into the buffers; when you read again, DOS consults the buffers to learn if the data are already there.

Each buffer takes up 528 bytes (or more, under some disk-partitioning software running under DOS version 2 or 3), so, if you have, say, 20 buffers, they will consume 10,560 bytes of memory.

How many buffers are enough? You should follow recommendations that come with your application. Another hint: If, while a program is performing some repetitious disk operation, such as reading through a list of files, disk accesses suddenly grow slow, available buffer space has been exhausted.

If you are using a disk cache, it will largely supplant the DOS buffers. You can then follow the cache maker's recommendation of how many buffers to leave.

Apart from how many total buffers you have, when should you call upon QEMM to load them into upper memory? This depends mostly on what version of DOS you have:

✗ Under DOS versions 2 and 3, QEMM buffers are appropriate whenever you have upper memory available.

✗ If you use DOS 4, you're out of luck, because QEMM does not support the buffers format under this version. Note also that, if you use the /X parameter to load buffers into expanded memory, you may face compatibility problems with many forms of software.

✗ Under DOS 5, the best solution is to use DOS=HIGH, which loads buffers into the High Memory Area. When you use QEMM-386, up to 51 buffers can coexist with the DOS kernel in the HMA. If you then use LOADHI buffers as well, the original buffers in the HMA will go to waste. If you don't use DOS=HIGH, you can use LOADHI BUFFERS as you would for DOS 2 or 3.

To use QEMM's buffers, follow these steps:

1. Reduce the value on the BUFFERS line in CONFIG.SYS to read BUFFERS=1, to compel DOS to reduce its buffers to a minimum.

2. Place a LOADHI command near the top of your AUTOEXEC.BAT file (before any program is loaded that will need to use buffers). Enter, for instance,

loadhi buffers=40

to create a total of 40 buffers. You can also phrase this command "loadhi buffers=+39." If you place this command before your PATH command, you will have to precede both LOADHI and BUFFERS with the complete path to your QEMM directory. Or, better, simply add the line **buffers=40** or **buffers=+39** to AUTOEXEC.BAT and then run OPTIMIZE to allow it to add LOADHI commands with the optimal parameters.

3. Reboot and enter **qemm list** to verify that the buffers have been loaded into upper memory.

Files

The FILES line creates a system resource—file handles—used by DOS and newer DOS applications to refer to open disk files (those currently in use). Five of these handles are normally always open and normally refer to system entities: standard input and standard output (high-level references to your keyboard and screen), standard error (for displaying error messages), as well as handles usually referring to a serial port and a parallel printer port. You need enough file handles at the outset to attach to all these devices plus as many files as your programs may have open at a given time. Note that resident programs as well as programs in a multi-tasking environment may keep files open. A file handle takes only about 60 bytes of memory.

To use QEMM's FILES command, reduce the value on your FILES line in CONFIG.SYS to read FILES=10 (FILES=15 if you use Windows). Certain applications demand that some of the original handles be available. Enter a line such as **files=30** near the top of

AUTOEXEC.BAT and run OPTIMIZE, to yield a total of 30 file handles. Reboot to verify.

FCBs

You can ignore this section if either of these conditions is true:

✗ You don't have an FCBS= line in your CONFIG.SYS file.

✗ You don't use the DOS SHARE command.

File control blocks (FCBs) are an old device for regulating access to disk files; only programs written before the advent of DOS 2 use them. If you use any such applications, you can relocate these blocks (each of which consumes 53 bytes of memory) by removing the FCBS statement from CONFIG.SYS (after noting the figures that follow) and adding a command **fcbs=*n,n*** to your AUTOEXEC.BAT file, using the original FCBS values for *n,n*. Follow the same steps given in the previous section for using BUFFERS (including running OPTIMIZE).

LASTDRIVE

DOS maintains a table of characteristics for each logical drive (a disk drive designated by a letter name) in your system. There must be at least as many such structures as you have drives, but, if there are more, some memory is wasted. If you have more than the default number of drives for your version of DOS, you must use the LASTDRIVE line.

If you use this line, you can save a little bit of conventional memory by using the QEMM equivalent. To do this, set the original LASTDRIVE line in CONFIG.SYS to the last physical drive in your system. (For instance, if you have a single hard disk, set it to LASTDRIVE=C.) Then, add a line to your AUTOEXEC.BAT file in the form **lastdrive** *x*, where *x* is the highest drive letter that you use (including RAM disks and network drives). Finally, run OPTIMIZE. Follow the general directions for BUFFERS above.

CREATING MORE CONVENTIONAL MEMORY WITH VIDRAM

VIDRAM is a resident program that steals from your EGA or VGA graphics memory to add to your conventional memory. You may be able to use it if you seldom or never run a program in graphics mode (this obviously leaves out a program like Windows), if you have a full 640K of physical conventional memory, and if your hardware and software are compatible with VIDRAM.

VIDRAM adopts one of two strategies for obtaining the extra address space:

✗ It can scavenge video graphics RAM directly for use as conventional memory. This approach leaves the most system memory available, but it leads to slow access (video RAM is rather slow) and more frequent compatibility problems.

✗ It can map extended RAM to replace the video RAM. This is the more conservative approach and the fastest, but it consumes extended memory.

To try out VIDRAM, follow these steps:

1. Use QEMM or Manifest to make sure that you don't have programs loaded between B000 and B7FF (including QEMM-386). If there are such programs, remove their LOADHI commands. Remove an R:*n* parameter from QEMM386.SYS if it refers to this region. The VIDRAM parameters will block use of this area as upper memory.

2. Add the parameter VIDRAMEGA or VIDRAMEMS to the QEMM386 line in CONFIG.SYS. The former option tells VIDRAM to use graphic adapter memory; the letter tells it to use extended memory. You can try first one, then the other.

3. Add the line **vidram on** to your AUTOEXEC.BAT file.

4. Reboot and enter **mem** to see how your conventional memory has increased.

You should try out your usual applications, even those that appear to use text mode only, for compatibility. If some programs don't handle the screen properly, you can turn off VIDRAM as you run them. The simplest method is to write a batch file with these contents:

```
@echo off
vidram off
d:\path\name
vidram on
```

Make your current working directory one that appears earlier on your path than your application. Create the file in this directory using a text editor such as DOS's MS-DOS Editor or Windows' Notepad and name it after your application, on the pattern NAME.BAT.

You can save about 1.6K of conventional memory by loading VIDRAM into upper memory. Here's a small trick: Instead of adding one line to AUTOEXEC.BAT, add two.

```
vidram resident
vidram on
```

Run OPTIMIZE to add the appropriate LOADHI command before the first of these lines.

OTHER QEMM PROGRAMS

The QEMM package offers some small programs that offer further uses for expanded memory:

✗ The EMS2EXT program allows you to make memory on an EMS board available as raw extended memory, for use by a few programs that use extended memory but do not address it directly, such as VDISK. To use it, place the line

device=c:\qemm\ems2ext.sys memory=*nnn speed*

in your CONFIG.SYS file. For *nnn,* specify the number of kilobytes that you wish to allocate. For *speed,* specify FAST or SLOW (or nothing). Use the setting that works best.

✗ The EMS.COM program offers some control over how EMS is provided, whether by QEMM386.SYS or an EMS board. You can enter **ems** at the command line for a report on how much expanded memory you have installed, how much is free, and where the page frame is located. You can enter **ems dir** for a report on the pages of memory assigned to each handle, the number of kilobytes assigned to each handle, and the name assigned to the handle, if any. Other options to EMS.COM are for the use of software designers, for testing purposes.

By now, you have QEMM installed and know how to interpret and work with its basic diagnostic tools, reports, and screen maps. You are ready to use Manifest, QEMM's versatile reporting tool, to explore your system and to work with its powerful Analysis function to solve problems and make the best possible use of upper memory. These topics, plus notes on configuring QEMM to work with some popular programs and hardware configurations, are taken up in the next chapter.

CHAPTER SIX

USING

QEMM

The QEMM package includes a comprehensive guide to what's going on under the cover of your PC, called Manifest. This chapter is an introduction to Manifest, its screens and recommendations. The all-important Analysis feature (shared with QEMM.COM), which allows you to identify problems and opportunities in upper memory use, is covered in this chapter. Finally, this chapter features a roundup of special compatibility issues for QEMM and further resources for troubleshooting.

USING MANIFEST

Manifest can operate like any application that you start, use, and then exit (in other words, as a transient program) or can operate as a TSR. Because it occupies about 120K of memory, you may not want to load it as a TSR routinely (unless you have that much extra upper memory in which to load it). Instead, make it resident, test the memory requirements and other behavior of an application, and then remove it.

To operate Manifest as a transient program, with MFT.EXE on your DOS PATH (it should be in your QEMM directory), enter

mft

at the DOS command line. The System Overview screen should come up. Note that the menu running down the left side is the primary menu. The one across the top is subsidiary; its contents change as you choose new main menu items. Thus, you choose first a left-hand item like System, then a top item like Overview.

Choose a menu item in one of these ways:

✗ Press arrow keys until the item is marked by wedges (left menu) or highlighted (top menu).

✗ Type the highlighted letter for the desired item.

✗ Move the diamond-shaped mouse pointer to the desired item and click on it (if you have a mouse).

To exit Manifest, press Esc twice. To terminate the program but keep it resident, however, press Esc (or select Exit), select Stay Resident, and press the key combination that you would like to use as a hot key from those listed. Thereafter, you can alternately pop up Manifest and return to your application by pressing that key combination. You can also start Manifest in resident mode by adding the /T parameter to the command line; you can then pop up and "unpop" the program by pressing the default hot-key combination, Left Shift-Left Ctrl.

You can run Manifest in black and white (which might result in a clearer display on an LCD monitor) by starting it with the /M parameter. You can start it at a particular screen by forming a parameter consisting of the highlighted letter for the main category plus the highlighted letter for the subsidiary screen, such as QM for the QEMM-386 Memory screen. Other parameters are listed in the command reference in Chapter 7.

Manifest screens are listed in the sections that follow, one by one. You may find it useful as you read to tour these screens yourself in Manifest. Note that you can see a brief synopsis of the information on a screen by pressing F1; pressing the key again returns you to the original screen. You can send the contents of a screen (or a series of screens, or all screens) to a printer on your LPT1 port or to a file by pressing F2 and highlighting choices from the menus you see.

System Screens

System screens get the information they display from a combination of hardware tests and data provided by your PC's BIOS and CMOS. If either of these latter elements is organized in a nonstandard way, Manifest information may not be accurate.

Overview

The Overview screen shows basic information about your PC's configuration, as well as about installed memory and free memory (conventional memory, raw extended memory, and expanded memory). Note the BIOS date information: This is useful in determining if your BIOS is the source of compatibility problems and in need of an update.

CONFIG

The CONFIG screen shows the contents of your current CONFIG.SYS file; if the file is longer than one screen can hold, you will be prompted to press PgDn to see more. Watch for notices like these at the bottom of many Manifest screens as signs that there is more to see.

AUTOEXEC

The AUTOEXEC screen shows the contents of your current AUTOEXEC.BAT file.

Adapter

Successive screens display the video display, disk drive, and serial/parallel adapters on your system.

Note the addresses in upper memory occupied by your video display. They may read like these figures for a video adapter, for instance:

```
Video Memory: A000 - AFFF Graphics
              B800 - BFFF Text
Video ROM:    C000 - C7FF
```

"Video Memory" is video RAM. Note the gap between graphics and text memory, which QEMM can fill with RAM. Note also that text RAM and ROM are contiguous. If you have a specialized video adapter, the addresses may be different. If the manual for your adapter shows use of addresses that QEMM has not detected, these addresses may be candidates for exclusion. Note the type number for your hard-disk drive on the next screen. This is a figure that you should have down on paper somewhere, in case you ever have problems with your hard drive and this value, taken from CMOS, is lost.

The last screen shows port addresses for serial and parallel adapters, as well as current values for some important serial and parallel lines, useful for diagnosing problems with, for instance, communications software.

CMOS

CMOS (which stands for complementary metal-oxide semiconductor) is a special form of memory where your PC stores its system configuration. The values are preserved from one session to another by a battery. If the battery dies, the values are lost and your PC's BIOS will reset them to their defaults on boot-up.

The value that you are most likely to scramble to locate, the hard-disk-type number, occurs again on this screen. Small shareware utilities are available to save the entire contents of your CMOS to disk and to restore it again.

The initial screen shows the most commonly used values, which are refreshed each time you bring up this screen. (You can observe how the Time value changes.) You can see a more detailed listing by pressing F3, the standard Manifest key for alternate listings. Pressing F3 a second time returns you to the original screen.

First Meg Screens

This series of screens covers DOS memory: its contents and makeup. Note that, if you start Manifest from an environment such as DESQview or Windows enhanced mode, you will see the contents of the DOS session created in V86 mode by the environment, not the original DOS session.

Overview

The Overview screen classifies the contents of DOS memory, rather like the QEMM TYPE screen. The area above the Conventional Memory line on the screen (below it in terms of address space) classifies the lower 640K:

✗ The interrupt area, BIOS data area, and system data areas are maintained by your BIOS (as modified by programs) and are on the screens described below.

✗ The DOS area is occupied by your DOS kernel and detailed on the DOS Overview and DOS Drivers screens.

✗ The program area is memory occupied by part of COMMAND.COM and by resident programs loaded when you run Manifest.

✗ The remaining memory is available. Manifest does not subtract the memory that it occupies itself.

The remainder of the screen classifies upper memory by type, much as you saw QEMM TYPE do. The High Memory Area, if engaged by your memory manager, will be shown at the bottom of the last screen.

Programs

The Programs screen, shown in Figure 6.1, displays all the programs in conventional or remapped upper memory (device drivers, resident programs, or shells, such as COMMAND.COM), with their locations and sizes. Available areas of memory are also displayed. Available memory below 640K (shown above the legend "Conventional memory ends at 640K") is available for your applications. Available areas in upper memory may provide homes for device drivers and TSRs. The memory manager

FIGURE 6.1: *Manifest First Meg programs*

QEMM386.SYS must be loaded for Manifest to display the contents of upper memory. Manifest does not list itself unless it is resident (and thus likely to affect space available for your next application).

Interrupts

The first Interrupts screen shows programs that initially receive an interrupt—where they begin in memory, what they are named, and what interrupts they receive. The alternate screen, which you reach by pressing F3, shows the interrupt table that occupies the bottom 1K of memory. Interrupt vectors appear in ascending numerical order. Each is shown with the address where it leads (which begins a programming entity called an "interrupt service routine") and the process that occupies that address (system or other ROM, a driver or resident program, or an application).

Interrupts are a fairly technical subject; if you don't already understand them, this screen is unlikely to help you much. If you do, you may find it helpful in avoiding conflicts among programs.

INTERRUPTS

Interrupts are a means to grab the attention of the CPU immediately, not by following the normal flow of processor instructions. An application itself may use interrupts. For instance, a communications program may install an interrupt handler to deal with characters coming along the serial line.

The alternative is the technique called *polling*, in which the program checks every so often for a new incoming character. Given rapid communications rates, if this technique were used, it would be liable to miss characters. Using interrupts, each incoming character signals the processor to interrupt what it is doing (and save the prior context) and run the routine to process the character.

TSRs need keyboard interrupt handler routines. When the keyboard controller announces that a key has been pressed or released, the first keyboard handler routine is called. It may check to see if the key is its hot key (in conjunction with the states of the Shift keys)—its signal to pop up. It should then pass the keystroke value on to the next keyboard interrupt handler. In this way, several handler routines (from the running application, one or more TSRs, and, finally, the BIOS) can be lined up to have their chance to process a keystroke.

Several interrupts are controlled by hardware, such as the one initiated by the keyboard controller itself.

The CPU responds to an interrupt by reading an entry from the interrupt vector table at the bottom of memory, which has an entry for each interrupt beginning from 0. (This is the table you see when you press F3 at the First Meg Interrupts screen.) The content of the entry is the starting address of the first handler routine for that interrupt, which is then given control of the processor. (Manifest supplies the numbers and names of the interrupts and the names of processes running at the target addresses.)

BIOS Data

The BIOS data area is a 172-byte region just above the interrupt vector table, where the BIOS and cooperating programs maintain data about the current machine environment. (These include how much conventional memory is installed, I/O addresses for serial and parallel ports, the current text screen dimensions, and so on.)

The BIOS data area screen is chiefly of interest to programmers and other technical users, who will understand its uses.

Timings

The Timings screen tests the speed of any memory (RAM or ROM) found in the first megabyte. Timings appear as multiples of the speed of RAM in a classic 4.77-MHz IBM PC/XT. Timings are subject to a small variation and are updated each time you select this screen.

If your PC has a hardware cache, a separate timing for cache memory should also appear here. This screen can identify bottlenecks in your system memory. (For instance, video memory is usually a bottleneck. If it is very slow, you might benefit from a faster video card. If you have ROM that has not been shadowed, you can see the benefits of replacing it with RAM, using built-in ROM shadowing or QEMM's ROM parameter). Finally, if any of your conventional memory is slower than your extended memory (as shown by shadow RAM or the HMA), you may gain from allowing QEMM to sort your memory, by omitting the NOSORT parameter.

Remember that sorting is incompatible with Windows enhanced mode and certain other programs.

Expanded Memory Screens

This series of screens describes the form of expanded memory in use. If there is no expanded memory (for instance, if you have the NOEMS parameter on the QEMM386 line), the Overview screen will read "None!" and no other screens will be available.

Overview

If there is expanded memory, the Overview screen names the manager providing it, its EMS version, where the page frame is located, and how many mappable pages are available. Below, it describes how much expanded memory has been created, how much is free, how many handles (designations for EMS clients to request blocks of memory) exist and are free, and how many alternate maps (used by DESQview) exist and are free.

Pages

The Pages screen, shown in Figure 6.2, shows a map of DOS memory viewed in terms of EMS. It is narrower than other such maps because EMS uses memory in 16K blocks instead of in 4K blocks. Thus, four columns make up a 64K line. The detailed portion at the upper right shows where EMS page numbers fall into this space. Remember that pages 0 through 3 make up the page frame.

Handles

Each process requesting expanded memory is given a handle, which is a sequential number. The Handles screen shows these handles, the amount of memory assigned to each one, their sizes, and their names, if any.

This screen can give you a sense of how many expanded memory users you have and how much memory they are demanding. The definition of expanded memory is a bit broad in this context; XMS and protected-mode clients receive handle

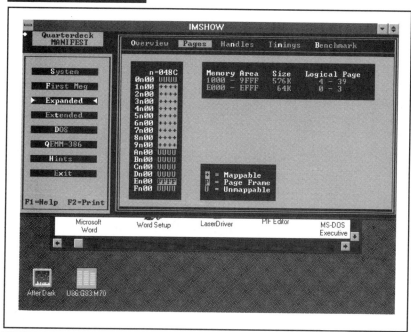

FIGURE 6.2: *The Pages screen, showing Manifest EMS pages*

numbers, as do EMS users. Remember that Handle 0 always refers to mappable conventional memory and so is owned by the memory manager itself, as is a handle named for the HMA.

Timings

The Timings screen shows speeds of memory being assigned as EMS (or XMS). The standard is the same as for First Meg timings.

Benchmark

The Benchmark screen shows the speed of your EMS memory as it is put through a series of representative operations. The values are continuously updated. If you have access to more than one Expanded Memory Manager, you can use this test to compare them. (The lower the numbers, the better.) Otherwise, this material is of interest to programmers.

Extended Memory Screens

The first of this pair of screens shows use of raw extended memory. The second shows memory made available through the memory manager as XMS memory.

Overview

The Overview screen shows who is using raw extended memory. Each user receives a line describing the addresses assigned, the size of the area, and how the user has allocated this memory. (For instance, QEMM will show the status "Used from Top," meaning that it assigns extended memory from the highest address downward.) Memory that is not in use (for instance, that you have prevented QEMM from using with the /EXTMEM= parameter) will be shown as "Available." If you have assigned all extended memory to QEMM, the breakdown will consist of one line. The sizes shown here should add up to the memory in use in your system, minus conventional memory, shadow RAM, RAM mapped to upper memory, and top memory.

If a known extended memory user is not shown on this screen, the program using extended memory through the back door in this way is likely to create problems for QEMM, Windows, and other legitimate users (by being invisible to them). You would do well to change its operating parameters or to find a more modern replacement.

XMS

The XMS screen will appear only if your memory manager is making XMS available. (You can prevent QEMM386.SYS from doing this by giving it the NOXMS parameter.) It shows the XMS version and driver revision, use of the High Memory Area, use of the A20 line (if it is not enabled, the HMA is not available as DOS memory), and the number of handles available, which should agree with the number of available handles shown on the

Expanded Overview screen. It also shows how much total RAM in upper memory (this screen gets the terminology right!) is free and shows the largest contiguous block that is free. You can use this information to help you arrange upper memory to load yet another program. It shows the same information for XMS extended memory.

DOS Screens

The DOS series of screens shows aspects of how DOS is configured on your system.

Overview

The Overview screen shows your DOS version and the sizes of system areas, including the kernel (IO.SYS and MSDOS.SYS, when loaded in memory, including the irreducible minimum of file handles and buffers), base data (DOS resources created by DOS itself), and added data (DOS resources in conventional memory created by DOS SHARE or QEMM). The exact total numbers of DOS resources are shown next. The right area of the screen shows exactly where each of these areas falls in memory, its size, and whether it occupies conventional memory or upper memory.

Drivers

The Drivers screen shows strictly technical information on all device drivers, built-in or added through CONFIG.SYS.

Files

The Files screen shows how many file handles and file control blocks are on your system and how many are open (that is, in use). You can also see the names associated with open file handles: standard names like AUX and PRN, or the names of programs or files that the handles belong to.

158 USING QEMM

CHAPTER SIX

You can use this screen (especially with Manifest resident) to see if you have enough file handles for your applications, or if you could save some memory by reducing an excessive number of file handles.

Environment

The Environment screen is a listing of strings in your DOS environment, similar to what you see if you type **set** at a DOS command prompt. Each string equates some term (called an *environment variable*) with some value; for instance, the term "PATH" will be equated with a list of disk drives and directories that DOS will search for programs to execute, and the term "PROMPT" will be equated with a sequence of characters used to produce the DOS command-line prompt. Environment strings may be written and read by DOS, your applications, or yourself—users often manipulate them, for instance, to produce sophisticated batch files.

The environment is assigned a fixed amount of memory when COMMAND.COM is first loaded; this amount must be enough to hold all the environment strings that are produced. If there is a large amount free, you may be able to reduce the environment size. On the other hand, some programs may load and then remove several environment variables as they work. (Installation programs often do this.) You may therefore need a larger environment than is apparent. The size is given as an argument to the line in CONFIG.SYS that loads COMMAND.COM; for instance, the line

```
shell=c:\command.com /e:512 /p
```

creates an environment of 512 bytes. If there is no such line, an environment is created of the default size for your operating-system version (256 bytes for DOS 5).

QEMM-386 Screens

The whole series of QEMM-386 screens appears only if you are using QEMM-386 and if it is visible to Manifest (for instance, not when you start the program from Windows enhanced mode, which runs Manifest in a Windows-created V86 machine environment). It includes the all-important screens that describe how QEMM is treating DOS memory, how much is being used, and how this usage squares with QEMM's expectations of available memory.

Overview

The Overview screen shows you the QEMM version and sub-version number, the QEMM status—that is, what the program is doing (such as creating RAM in upper memory and mapping ROM)—whether the program is on or off (in or out of V86 mode), and the location of the page frame.

Type

The two Type screens (selected by pressing F3) are identical to the QEMM TYPE and QEMM TYPE MAP screens described in Chapter 5. That is, they show the different types of memory in the first megabyte address space, by 4K increments.

> *If you are unsure how to read these screens, you are urged to review the material under the headings "DOS Memory Types" and "DOS Memory Maps" in Chapter 5.*

Like the QEMM TYPE displays, you can use these screens to find where your resident programs are being placed and where the unused spaces are, as an aid to juggling and consolidating free upper memory. One obvious use is to make sure that the page frame is located in upper memory.

Accessed

The two Accessed screens, a listing and a map, are selected by pressing F3. You can see the same information by entering QEMM ACC or QEMM ACC MAP from the command line. They identify areas of DOS memory that have been read or written since any of various events have happened (QEMM was loaded, an area of memory was remapped, the page frame was cleared, or you entered a QEMM RESET command). With these caveats, these screens can help you track use of memory. Note that QEMM and Manifest take care to leave no footprints of their own on these screens.

Blocks of memory are described as "unaccessed," "accessed" (which means "read but not written"), and "written." The map uses the abbreviations U, A, and W.

One simple use is to see how much conventional memory an application occupies. Follow this sequence:

1. Enter **qemm reset** from a DOS prompt.

2. Enter **mft qa** and note the highest address in conventional memory that has been accessed or written.

3. Start your application and perform a usual sequence of actions. (The amount of memory an application demands may depend on the functions that you exercise, the size of data objects, such as documents, and other factors.)

4. Exit the application and run **mft qa** again. Note the new high-water mark and subtract the difference. You can convert the result to decimal numbers, if you like, using the techniques given in Appendix A.

The Accessed screen is also one means of uncovering unused upper address space that can be reclaimed for RAM. A more direct technique, analysis, is covered below.

Analysis

The two Analysis screens (a listing and a map, corresponding to QEMM AN and QEMM AN MAP) compare actual memory usage with expectations reflected on the QEMM386 line (explicit I= and X= parameters, and other parameters affecting memory use). Values shown here are meaningful only in connection with the analysis procedure described below.

Memory

The Memory screen duplicates the QEMM MEM screen described in Chapter 5; that is, it shows the whole picture of how QEMM is disposing your system's memory and how much it is using for its own needs.

DESQview Screens

The two screens in the DESQview series appear only when you start Manifest under DESQview, Quarterdeck's multitasking windowing environment for DOS applications or special, dedicated applications.

Overview

The Overview screen displays the DESQview version as well as figures describing the size and placement of the window in which Manifest itself is running.

Memory Status

The Memory Status screen shows total amounts, total availabilities, and largest available contiguous blocks for three kinds of memory available under DESQview: common memory (used by DESQview itself and by DESQview applications), conventional memory, and expanded memory (made available by a memory manager, including XMS memory).

Hints

Hints are suggestions from Manifest that may allow you to make more memory available or otherwise make more efficient use of your system. They are inferred from results shown on other screens. These hints may or may not be appropriate to your situation; it is up to you to determine whether they will work. Some of these hints, with their included commentaries, should be self-evident. This section lists some that deserve further comment.

Stop loading HIMEM.SYS

HIMEM.SYS still appears in your CONFIG.SYS file. There is rarely any reason to use it in conjunction with QEMM. (It may precede QEMM to use all the memory on certain Compaq-clone EISA machines with more than 16MB of memory.) You should edit it out of the file.

Reduce the number of DOS FILES allocated

Try making Manifest resident and loading as many resident programs and applications as you use at one time. You can pop up Manifest and inspect the DOS Files screen described previously to see if you have a large surplus of free file handles. In this case, edit CONFIG.SYS (and AUTOEXEC.BAT, if you are using the QEMM FILES resource) to reduce the number of files to the number you use, plus a few more as a reserve. Increase the number if any application produces FILES-related error messages.

Reduce the number of DOS BUFFERS allocated

Increasing the number of buffers beyond a level leads to diminishing returns at the expense of memory and leads to increasing time spent searching through buffers. If you have many more than, perhaps, 30 buffers (from DOS or as a QEMM resource), try reducing them and see if performance suffers.

Consider using a good disk cache. The cache documentation will probably tell you to reduce the buffers to some small number, and the cache will easily outperform the buffers. You may want to leave 10 or 15 buffers even if the cache documentation suggests a smaller number. In this way, you always have a useful buffering effect, even when you have disabled the cache during, say, disk backups or defragmentation.

Reduce your DOS environment size

Bring up the Manifest DOS Environment screen and see if you have a lot of free space in your environment. If so, edit (or create) the SHELL line in CONFIG.SYS to reduce it to the size needed.

It may be that, during certain operations, much more environment space is in use than when you ran Manifest. Watch for "out of environment space" error messages.

Stop allocating
DOS STACKS in your CONFIG.SYS

Stacks are areas for temporary retention of data. In PCs, the stack begins at the very top of the area allotted to it. When an item is to be added to a stack, the register that holds the active stack location (called the *stack pointer*) is first set to the next lower address in memory, and then the item is copied to that location. This sequence is called pushing the stack. When the data are wanted, the stack is read and shrunk (this is called *popping*) in the precise reverse order. Think of the way trays are stored in a cafeteria (except that, in a PC, the stack is upside down). If a stack grows too large, it runs into memory used for some other purpose, and disaster strikes suddenly.

Applications as well as resident programs and drivers use stacks. In DOS versions prior to 3.3, when a program or driver interrupted a program, it would borrow the application's stacks. Because one could not predict how much room was left on that stack, later DOS versions allowed creation of stacks for the use of DOS and resident programs. By default, nine stacks are formed having 128 bytes each (taking up 1168 bytes of conventional memory).

You remove these stacks—thus taking back this small amount of conventional memory—by setting your STACKS line in CONFIG.SYS to read

```
stacks=0,0
```

But this is hazardous. Some applications (including Windows), in fact, need larger than default stacks to work reliably. In these cases, you would do better to double the size of the default stacks by using the line

```
stacks=9,256
```

Run the OPTIMIZE program which came with QEMM

Manifest has detected something less than optimal in how your programs are arranged in memory. Try rerunning OPTIMIZE as described in Chapter 5 to see if your current arrangement can be improved. If you have consciously prevented OPTIMIZE from taking some action, such as loading a particular program into upper memory, you can ignore this hint.

Make QEMM your first driver in CONFIG.SYS

When QEMM386.SYS is loaded first, it has the greatest control over your PC's memory, and you have the opportunity to load following drivers high.

Occasionally, however, a driver may not work unless it is loaded first. Or, you may have a disk driver (such as the one used for compressing data on disk) that must be loaded before your QEMM directory can be read. In this case, you must load the disk driver first (or, better, reinstall QEMM on the uncompressed drive).

Fix the Token Ring/expanded memory conflict

Try adding an X= statement to your QEMM386 line, excluding the area shown on screen from QEMM's use. If no area is shown (or if this doesn't work), use the Analysis feature described next to identify the memory region used by your network card, and exclude it.

IDENTIFYING MEMORY CONFLICTS AND OPPORTUNITIES

Sometimes, QEMM may err in locating RAM and ROM in your upper memory area. This error may be one of omission or one of commission. Here are its three most common forms:

✗ QEMM may think that an area of ROM is shorter than it is in reality, because the ROM has incorrectly identified its own length. It may then map RAM over the apparently unused area.

✗ QEMM may mistake an area of adapter RAM for free address space, because the RAM was unused at boot time, with the same result.

✗ QEMM may avoid mapping over ROM or RAM that is never actually used during a normal session.

The first two cases lead to conflicts and possible lockups or apparent equipment failures as needed code is mapped out or overwritten. The last case represents an opportunity, a chance to wring more space out of your upper memory. This section covers the means to uncover these cases.

Your Diagnostic Tools

The diagnostic tool here may be QEMM.COM or Manifest, interchangeably. You can choose the more bare-bones utility, which uses less memory, or you can have fancier screens with more help available. This section uses QEMM commands in its examples. Table 6.1 shows the correspondences between the two sets of commands.

You must use QEMM RESET to clear memory in either case.

TABLE 6.1: *QEMM and Manifest Analysis Commands*

	ACCESSED LIST	ACCESSED MAP	ANALYSIS LIST	ANALYSIS MAP
QEMM.COM Parameters	ACC	ACC MAP	AN	AN MAP
Manifest Keys	Q A F3	Q A	Q N F3	Q N

INVESTIGATING CONFLICTS IN UPPER MEMORY

There are actually several ways to investigate conflicts in your upper memory. One of these may be simpler for you than using the Analysis feature or may be necessary if, for some reason, analysis fails.

Consult the manuals for your hardware devices (especially add-on cards) and find what memory addresses they use. See if these conflict with uses shown on the Manifest QEMM- 386 Type screen. Either have the cards use other addresses (by setting jumpers) or add X= parameters to the QEMM386 line to cover the areas used.

Exclude all of upper memory (with a parameter X=A000-FFFF) or any suspect part of it (for example, with a parameter X=C000-EFFF). If this solves your problem, cut the excluded area in half and repeat. If this doesn't work, try excluding the other half. Continue narrowing down excluded memory to the narrowest area possible. Note that you can have more than one EXCLUDE parameter on the QEMM386 line.

Running an Analysis

To analyze your system, take these steps, which apply whether you are tracking a conflict or looking for additional memory to include:

1. Edit your QEMM386 line in CONFIG.SYS: Remove the RAM parameter and add an ON parameter, to make sure that QEMM386 is running but not using upper memory.

2. Reboot your system.

3. Exercise your system. If some new piece of hardware or software is causing the problem, you may need only exercise all its normal functions to make sure that it uses the problem address range. If you are unsure of the source of

your problems, however, exercise your whole system. Use your ingenuity to try to activate all ROM BIOS and device code. Run software over a network. Search for a file on your hard disk. Format a floppy disk. Print something. Turn on your communications program and initialize your modem. Run all your customary software, using different video modes. (Avoid Windows enhanced mode, however, as it may bias results.)

4. Enter **qemm an** or **qemm an map**. The latter will show a report something like the one shown in Figure 6.3.

Any I's and X's represent memory use contrary to QEMM's expectations: X's are addresses unexpectedly used (and that, presumably, should be excluded), and I's are addresses unexpectedly unused (that may be included).

```
      n=0123 4567 89AB CDEF
0n00  0000 0000 0000 0000
1n00  0000 0000 0000 0000
2n00  0000 0000 0000 0000
3n00  0000 0000 0000 0000
4n00  0000 0000 0000 0000
5n00  0000 0000 0000 0000
6n00  0000 0000 0000 0000    O = OK
7n00  0000 0000 0000 0000    X = Exclude
8n00  0000 0000 0000 0000    I = Include
9n00  0000 0000 0000 0000
An00  0000 0000 0000 0000
Bn00  0000 0000 0000 0000
Cn00  0000 0000 IIOI 0000
Dn00  0000 0000 0000 0000
En00  0000 0000 0000 0000
Fn00  OIII IIOI 0000 OIOO
```

FIGURE 6.3: *The QEMM AN MAP report*

In the map above, I's appear in the block C800-CBFF and in areas above F000. The first block is hard-disk BIOS; the marked areas may be used only for operations like initialization and low-level formatting of the drive. The other areas are in ROM BIOS and may likewise be used only for machine setup.

5. Remove the ON parameter from the QEMM386 line, restore the RAM parameter, and add parameters for new exclusions (EXCLUDE=, or simply X=) and inclusions (INCLUDE=, or simply I=). A complete set of inclusions for the area above, for example, would run

    I=C800-C9FF I=CB00-CBFF I=F100-F5FF I=F700-F7FF
    I=FD00-FDFF

6. Reboot, run OPTIMIZE, and test the new settings thoroughly.

7. If you still have problems, run the sequence again, but, in step 1, add the parameter FR=NONE to remove the page frame. Its location might have caused the conflict.

8. If a program or device seems to access but not write unaccountably large areas, you can try including these areas (or all but the uppermost portion) to gain space. The device may merely be searching for its own code.

NOTE

Aggressive use of INCLUDES may not gain much memory if the contiguous spaces are small (less than 16K).

Watching Memory Access

At times, you may want to see simply how a program addresses memory, apart from QEMM's memory expectations. In this case, the QEMM ACCESSED (or ACC) command is used most simply.

An example is a resident program that insists on loading itself into upper memory, which you cannot relocate using

QEMM's LOADHI command, even with appropriate switches on its command line. A useful approach is to find out how much upper memory the program needs and then to clear upper RAM for it using the EXCLUDE parameter:

1. Edit the QEMM386 line to use the ON parameter instead of RAM, as in step 1 described in the previous section.

2. Reboot your system.

3. Enter **qemm acc map** and note upper memory use.

4. Load your program from the command prompt, pop it up, and use it as you do normally.

5. Enter **qemm acc map** again. Look for an added block of accessed or written memory and note its address range.

6. Restore the original QEMM386 line but add an X= parameter with that address range.

7. Reboot, use Manifest First Meg Programs to see that your program is in upper memory, and check its operation.

8. Add the program name to OPTIMIZE.EXC in your QEMM directory (if it isn't there already), restore the command to AUTOEXEC.BAT, and rerun OPTIMIZE.

FURTHER SOLUTIONS

The wealth of hardware and software available for the PC makes for an endless variety of fascinating compatibility problems. With your understanding of QEMM functioning, you may now be in a position to understand and solve many of them.

Conflicts with Stealth

Stealth works, basically, by removing ROM code from an area and remapping RAM into it. It then intercepts interrupts destined for that ROM code and redirects them to the new location. Thus, if a process seeks the ROM directly at its old address instead of via the interrupt, it will not find it there.

It is simple to tell if Stealth is implicated in a problem: Just remove the ST:M or ST:F parameter from the QEMM386 line and reboot. If the problem goes away, Stealth was involved. The steps to pinpoint a Stealth conflict are simple to follow but potentially long. You should obtain Quarterdeck's Technical Note #205, "Trouble-shooting Stealth," through their bulletin board system, CompuServe, or the mail. See "Help Is on the Line" later in this chapter to find how to connect directly with Quarterdeck.

 NOTE

The Stealth:F parameter will not work if the page frame location is fixed by an FR= parameter to QEMM386 and that place does not overlap ROM. In this case, you should remove FR=.

Conflicts with Windows

Most conflicts involving Windows occur with enhanced mode, generating error messages or causing Windows to fail to start. Here is a checklist of possible solutions to Windows problems:

✗ Make sure that you have QEMM version 5.10 or later (the later, the better). You can see the version number on Manifest's QEMM-386 Overview screen.

✗ Make sure that QEMM386.SYS has the parameters RAM, NOVIDEOFILL (or NV), and NOSORT (or NS). The NOVIDEOFILL parameter (among other functions) prevents QEMM's use of monochrome display memory, sometimes a bone of contention between QEMM and

Windows. Include NOFILL (NO) if you ordinarily backfill conventional memory. You can try the additional parameter NOSHADOWRAM (NOSH), which may make an improvement in some cases.

✗ If you have a PS/2 and QEMM version 5.10, add the NOXBDA parameter to the QEMM386 line.

✗ Try not loading DOS buffers or file handles into upper memory; use the normal FILES and BUFFERS lines in CONFIG.SYS instead.

✗ Try booting without unneeded device drivers and resident programs, especially those that use expanded memory.

✗ If the page frame is located at 9000, move it into upper memory by adding a parameter like FR=E000. (Use Manifest First Meg Programs to see where you have room.) This may involve creating more room in upper memory or using Stealth.

✗ Try a substitute for the NOVIDEOFILL parameter that will allow some shared use of the video area. Follow this sequence:

1. Find the Windows installation disk (#4) that has a file called MONOUMB2.38_.

2. Make your Windows directory current and enter **expand -r a:monoumb2.38_ c:\windows\system**, using the drive letter for your copy of Windows.

3. Add a line to the [386Enh] section of SYSTEM.INI reading **device=monoumb2.386**.

4. Try obtaining a variant form of this driver, called MONOUMB.386. Log onto CompuServe, reach the Microsoft Software library by entering **go msl,** choose to browse files, enter the keyword **monoumb,** and follow prompts to download the file you will see described, called MONO.EXE. From the DOS prompt and logged into your download directory, enter

> **mono.** Move the file MONOUMB.386 to your Windows SYSTEM subdirectory and make the changes listed above to SYSTEM.INI but substitute the name MONOUMB.386 for MONOUMB2.386. (See more notes on using CompuServe in the section "Help Is on the Line" at the end of this chapter.)

✗ Make sure that these lines also appear in the [386Enh] section of SYSTEM.INI:

SystemROMBreakPoint=false

VCPIWarning=false

✗ Try adding three additional lines to the [386Enh] section:

DualDisplay=True

EMMExclude=A000-CFFF

EMMExclude=E000-FFFF

Leave only those lines that are needed to make Windows work.

✗ Make sure that the file WINHIRAM.VXD (as well as WINSTLTH.VXD, if you use Stealth) appears in your QEMM directory. This file aids in an orderly transfer of power from QEMM to Windows enhanced mode. Try reinstalling the program to assure that you don't have a corrupted copy. Also, try obtaining the latest version of this file from Quarterdeck and see if there is any improvement. Add a parameter VXDDIR=C:\QEMM to your QEMM386 line, substituting your QEMM drive and directory.

Page Frame Location Problems

Some programs using EMS cannot locate a page frame that begins at E000 or higher. If your application reports that it can't find the frame, try moving it to D000 or lower using either the FR= parameter or Stealth. (You may have to move some device memory.)

Sticky Keys

Sticky Shift and other keys are usually caused by TSRs that spend too long handling keyboard interrupts. However, you may be able to alleviate the situation through QEMM. Try these measures:

✗ Tap the stuck key—this may unstick it.

✗ Unload your pop-ups one by one and see which one was responsible. Consider replacing it.

✗ Add the parameters IGNOREA20 (IA) and NOROM-HOLES (NRH) to the QEMM386 line. The A20 line that controls the High Memory Area shares a port address with the keyboard controller, and so, curiously, stopping QEMM from monitoring this line will reduce the overall overhead on the keyboard controller.

Exception 13 Errors

Exception 13's are error conditions that reveal themselves in a message like this:

> Exception #13 at xxxx:xxxx
>
> Error code 0
>
> Terminate, Reboot or Continue?

These messages are generated when QEMM detects a program trying to address memory not belonging to it. There may be a bug in the program, or there may be some other unfortunate combination of circumstances.

Diagnosis of Exception 13 problems is long and complex. You should obtain Quarterdeck Technical Note #232, "Exception #13 Advanced Troubleshooting," which will guide you through the task systematically.

"Packed File Corrupt" Errors

"Packed File Corrupt" error messages result from a bug in some programs that makes them unable to run in the bottom 64K of memory (something they were never called upon to do before you loaded all your TSRs into upper memory). To correct this, precede the line that loads the program with the DOS command LOADFIX.

PS/1 Machines

PS/1 computers come out of the box booting from CONFIG.SYS and AUTOEXEC.BAT files located in ROM. You must first reconfigure them to use system files on disk (which can then be modified like any others). From the opening screen, select first IBM DOS and then Customize How System Starts. Select the option from the following screen Try Diskette First, Then Try Fixed Disk. Select further to read CONFIG.SYS and AUTOEXEC.BAT "From Disk." Select C as the "Disk to Read From."

Set CONFIG.SYS to be read/write, rather than read only, by giving the command

```
c:\dos\attrib -r c:\config.sys
```

Next remove (or remark out by preceding with REM) a line in CONFIG.SYS that reads

```
INSTALL=C:\DOS\SHELLSTB.COM C:\DOS\ROMSHELL.COM
```

OPTIMIZE may halt prematurely, due to a system bug. When this happens, edit AUTOEXEC.BAT. Find a line at the end of the file that looks like

```
@C:\QEMM\OPTIMIZE /SEG:xxxx /B:C C:\QEMM\LOADHI.OPT
```

Follow it with a new line that reads simply

> VER

Close the file and run OPT2.BAT by entering

> c:\opt2.bat

to complete optimization.

Unrecognized Microchannel Adapters

QEMM depends on a text file, MCA.ADL, for descriptions of add-on cards for PS/2 and other microchannel PCs. You should get the latest edition of MCA.ADL from Quarterdeck (the bulletin board, CompuServe, or Tech Support); it should contain a description for your card.

XGA Video Problems

Three simple fixes will solve most problems with XGA video adapters:

✗ Upgrade to QEMM 6.01 or later.

✗ For an MCA machine, make sure that there is a two-line entry in MCA.ADL that reads

> 8FDB   XGA Video Adapter
>
> /NT

✗ If running Windows, locate the line

> display=xgavdd.386

in SYSTEM.INI and replace it with

> display=*vddvga

Problems with Disk Compression Programs

You can spare yourself most complications involving disk compression utilities, such as SuperStor and Stacker, by leaving drive C as your uncompressed boot drive and installing QEMM on drive C. Apart from this, you should refer to Quarterdeck Technical Note #214, "Using Stacker and QEMM," for help with Stacker, and the unnumbered technical note "The Optimize/Superstor Troubleshooting Guide" for help with SuperStor.

Using QEMM with DR DOS

QEMM will work well to extend the capabilities of the DR DOS operating system. There are some points to note in connection with DR DOS version 6:

✗ Include the lines HIDOS=ON and DEVICE=C:\DRDOS\ HIDOS.SYS (using your drive and path) in your CONFIG.SYS file to allow the operating-system kernel and resources (files, buffers, and so on) to be loaded into upper memory or the High Memory Area. Add the command HIBUFFERS to load buffers into the HMA. Include these lines after the line to load QEMM.

✗ Use LOADHI.SYS and LOADHI.COM in place of the DR DOS commands for loading drivers and resident programs into upper memory.

✗ Allow the DR DOS kernel, buffers, and SSTORDRV.SYS to load themselves high, using instructions for reserving areas for such programs. Better, instruct DR DOS and the buffers to use the HMA.

✗ Don't create multiple configuration files using the CHAIN command in DR DOS, but combine them into a single

CONFIG.SYS file. If you don't, OPTIMIZE will not read any but the first file.

✗ Remark out (with REM) a command in CONFIG.SYS to load DEVSWAP.COM. This may also entail changing references to drive C to drive D and vice versa. Put the command back into effect after you have run OPTIMIZE. See your DR DOS manual for more details on DEVSWAP.

HELP IS ON THE LINE

In addition to the phone and fax support listed in your manuals, Quarterdeck offers news, support files, and technical help online. One source for this support is Quarterdeck's bulletin board; another is CompuServe.

The Quarterdeck Bulletin Board

You can reach the Quarterdeck Bulletin Board by phoning (310) 314-3227. Set your modem for 8 data bits, no parity. After the usual sign-in questions, you can register by entering **open** at the main menu and answering further questions. You will be asked to enter your DESQview or QEMM serial number at a couple of points. After you have registered, you can join conferences, where you can receive direct technical support. You can also download white papers (technical notes), patches and upgrade files, and other files supporting QEMM and the DESQview environment. Many technical notes detail solutions to special problems using QEMM with given programs or environments. This is a typical bulletin board system; you can read more about using communications programs and computer bulletin boards in my *Up & Running with PROCOMM PLUS 2.0* (SYBEX, 1991) and *Understanding PROCOMM PLUS 2.0* (SYBEX, 1991).

CompuServe

Quarterdeck has its own forum on CompuServe, which you reach by entering **go quarterdeck**. Files and messages directly relevant to QEMM are concentrated in the Memory Management file and message sections. Many of the same files found on the bulletin board are also found in this file section. You need not register to use these areas—just join the forum by supplying your name.

Other CompuServe forums have message or file sections addressing memory management issues. For instance, you should check into the Windows Advanced Forum (GO WINADV) Memory Issues message and file sections for help with memory problems involving Windows. Try searching the Microsoft Knowledge Base (GO MSKB) and the Microsoft Library (GO MSL) for helpful documents and files. Search by keywords describing your area of interest.

You can learn how to use CompuServe from my book *Up & Running with CompuServe* (SYBEX, 1991).

This about covers the principles of troubleshooting with QEMM as well as solutions to some of the most common problems. Sometimes you can arrive at an ad hoc solution to a memory management problem or an improved use of memory just by scanning the options available and spotting the one most applicable to your situation. The next chapter covers all these options to the QEMM memory manager, as well as special options for loading programs into upper memory and for running the reporting program, Manifest.

CHAPTER SEVEN

QEMM

COMMAND

REFERENCE

QEMM must adapt to a great variety of software and hardware environments. It can do some of this on its own, but you can control QEMM by adding parameters to the command lines that load QEMM386.SYS, LOADHI, and Manifest. The astronomical number of possibilities for system configurations means that no set of cookbook solutions can cover every contingency. Sometimes you just have to try a parameter and see if it works. This chapter lists parameters alphabetically under each program.

QEMM386.SYS OPTIONS

Parameters to QEMM386.SYS consist of terms (single words or equations consisting of a word, an equal sign, and a value following the DEVICE=QEMM386.SYS line in CONFIG.SYS. Parameters are separated by spaces; no spaces should appear within an equation-type parameter. Letters may be uppercase or lowercase. Many parameter names have abbreviated forms; these appear in parentheses after the full name.

Parameters later in the line take precedence over those earlier in the line. For instance, you could place NOCOMPAQ-FEATURES on the line and follow it with COMPAQEGAROM to enable COMPAQEGAROM but disable other special Compaq features. In the absence of any explicit options, all Compaq features are enabled when QEMM detects that it is running on a Compaq PC.

Numerical values are in hexadecimal form. Four-digit values *nnnn* are typically hexadecimal values for segment addresses in DOS memory that you can obtain from QEMM.COM, Manifest, hardware or software documentation, or other sources.

You can use more than one instance of an equation-type parameter, using different values, for instance, X=B000-B7FF X=C000-CBFF. Use values that are multiples of 4K (that is, that mark the beginning and end of squares on a Manifest map screen—the start addresses end with two zeros, and the end addresses end with two F's). In most cases, when using Stealth, locating the page frame, or defining addresses otherwise involving EMS, you must define blocks of at least 16K (sets of four squares on a map screen). Start addresses at 16K boundaries are formed of an digit, followed by 0, 4, 8, or C, followed by two zeros. End addresses at 16K boundaries are formed of any digit, followed by 3, 7, B, or F, followed by two F's.

? Tells QEMM to list all available parameters.

ADAPTERRAM=*nnnn-nnnn* (ARAM)
You can also use the term ADAPTERROM=*nnnn-nnnn*. Tells QEMM not to use the given address range. These parameters work just like EXCLUDE, except that the QEMM and Manifest Type screens will show the areas as allocated to adapter RAM or adapter ROM, to help you document what is there.

AUTO (AU), ON, OFF (OF)
Runs QEMM in V86 mode (ON), real mode (OFF), or either mode (AUTO), depending on whether a program is requesting expanded memory. If the RAM or ROM switch is set, QEMM will always be set to ON regardless of these parameters.

COMPAQ386S (C386S)
Tells QEMM it is running on a Compaq 386S. This parameter is in lieu of running Compaq's setup program, version 6.02 or later, which will make this information available to QEMM.

COMPAQEGAROM (CER)
Has QEMM undo an action of the Compaq BIOS, which remaps video BIOS from C000 to RAM at E000; places the BIOS code in RAM mapped to C000 (as if by a ROM switch).

COMPAQHALFROM (CHR)   Has QEMM treat Compaq's two redundant blocks of ROM BIOS (at address ranges F000-F7FF and F800-FFFF) as separate so that one can be mapped over as RAM.

COMPAQROMMEMORY (CRM)   Has QEMM appropriate 128K of upper memory that Compaq uses to speed ROM BIOS and video ROM. QEMM can achieve the same result without using as much space.

The three preceding Compaq parameters are set as defaults when QEMM detects a Compaq PC. You can turn them off by using the parameter NOCOMPAQFEATURES (NCF).

DISKBUF=*nn* (DB)   Sets a size in kilobytes for the buffer used to transfer information to bus-mastering controllers (such as SCSI controllers) that don't have VDS drivers. (See Chapter 5.) Increasing the value makes for more efficient transfer, at the expense of conventional memory. A value of 10 may be a good starting point.

DISKBUFFRAME=*nn* (DBF)   Has QEMM buffer disk reads and writes that use the page frame directly. You normally add this parameter after QEMM gives you a message that it is needed. The kilobytes of memory specified by *nn* are taken from conventional memory; 10 is a reasonable value. A better solution than using this parameter is to configure your programs to use XMS instead of EMS.

DMA=*nnn* (DM)   Specifies a maximum size for the DMA (direct memory access) buffer, used by devices for direct access to memory, bypassing the CPU. The value *nnn* is in kilobytes and can range from 12 to 128. Some devices may need a larger size than the default (12K on most machines, but 64K on PS/2s); they will usually display an error message to tell you this.

DONTUSEXMS (DUX)   Tells QEMM not to call a previously loaded memory manager to request XMS memory (a rare situation).

DOS4 (D4)   Has QEMM adjust EMS page ordering to accommodate certain bugs in DOS version 4.

EMBMEM=*nnnn* (EM)   Tells QEMM to allow XMS users to see no more than *nnnn* kilobytes of XMS memory, leaving the rest of extended memory reserved for EMS, VCPI, or DPMI users. The default value is 12MB (12288K) according to the XMS specification. If you have more than 12MB of extended memory, and you *want* it all to be available as XMS, you should use this parameter and set the value to the amount of extended memory in your PC.

EXCLUDESTEALTH=*nnnn* (XST)   Tells Stealth not to relocate ROM beginning at address *nnnn,* perhaps because a process is trying to address ROM there directly, rather than through the interrupt table. Use this parameter after analyzing Stealth operation according to Quarterdeck's Technical Note #205, "Trouble-shooting Stealth."

EXCLUDESTEALTHINT=*nn* (XSTI)   Tells QEMM not to control interrupt *nn.* Reserve this parameter for dire needs; use it after working through the technical note described in the preceding entry.

EXTMEM=*nnnn* (EXT)   Tells QEMM to leave *nnnn* kilobytes of raw extended memory strictly alone, leaving it for primitive RAM disks and other software that uses raw memory. The inverse of this parameter is MEMORY=; you can specify the result either way—as how much to use or how much to leave alone.

EXCLUDE=*nnnn-nnnn* (E)   Tells QEMM not to use the given memory range. This usually describes an area of memory that Analysis (described in Chapter 6) found to be already used, although it had appeared to QEMM to be available. You may also see instructions to use EXCLUDE to avoid specific conflicts with software. If you are using Stealth, an excluded area will be broadened to the nearest boundaries that are multiples of 16K, unless you are inside an area defined by EXCLUDESTEALTH or, using Stealth:F, one that is outside the page frame.

EXCLUDESTEALTHINT=*nn* (XSTI)
Tells QEMM not to take control of an interrupt *nn* (a hexadecimal number) when using Stealth. Some programs may have expectations of how interrupts are handled that Stealth may violate. Try setting *nn* to 10 if you have problems with video display operations while using Stealth.

FASTINT10:N (F10)
Tells QEMM not to use its own replacements for some video BIOS (INT 10) routines. This may improve compatibility of the Stealth system; it is not useful otherwise.

FORCEEMS (FEMS)
Tells QEMM to act on requests for EMS memory, even if the page frame is shorter than 64K (as set by the FRAMELENGTH parameter).

FORCESTEALTHCOPY:Y (FSTC)
Tells QEMM to make copies of tables in ROM, even if the ROM is not being treated by Stealth. You use this parameter during Analysis when using Stealth, to give QEMM or Manifest enough information to avoid reporting that areas should be excluded when they need not be. Once you have made your configuration final, you should remove this parameter.

FRAME=*nnnn* (FR)
Specifies a starting address for the 64K EMS page frame; used when QEMM's own choice for an address is unsatisfactory. You should specify an address that is a multiple of 16K (a hexadecimal segment address that ends in 0, 4, 8, or C, and then at least two zeros) and that is followed by at least

64K of unused upper memory or of mappable conventional memory. If you specify FR=NONE, you put QEMM out of the business of being an Expanded Memory Manager (and you put Stealth out of business), but QEMM's other functions remain.

FRAMEBUF:Y/N (FB)   If you specify Y, reads or writes to or from the page frame are diverted through DOS buffers; if you specify N, they are more direct. When using Stealth, the Y value is the default.

FRAMELENGTH=*n* (FL)   Has QEMM set a page frame length of *n* pages, which can range from 0 to 4. Few programs can function with less than the default four pages, so this is a desperate space-saving measure whose results must be tested. The value *n*=0 is equivalent to FR=NONE. With values 1–3, add the FORCEEMS parameter.

GETSIZE (GS)   Has QEMM report the size it will occupy in memory, corresponding to LOADHI /GS. This parameter is intended for use by the OPTIMIZE program.

HANDLES=*nnn* (HA)   Specifies the number of handles available to expanded (and XMS) memory users, as a number between 16 and 255. Note that QEMM itself uses one or two handles.

HELP   Tells QEMM to display all parameters, with one-line descriptions.

HMAMIN=*nn*   Tells QEMM not to allow a program to use the High Memory Area unless it will use at least *nn* kilobytes of memory. This is to make most efficient use of the HMA when several programs have successive chances to claim it. Most often, you will have only one HMA user (usually DOS or DESQview), so this parameter is unnecessary.

IGNOREA20 (IA)   Tells QEMM not to trap the 8042 keyboard controller, that is, not to divert and monitor accesses to the corresponding range of I/O ports. This parameter disables support of HIMEM.SYS (which is very rarely useful with QEMM anyway) but may help solve keyboard problems, since the keyboard controller shares port addresses with the CPU's A20 line, which controls the High Memory Area.

INCLUDE=*nnnn-nnnn* (I)   Allows QEMM control of the range of memory specified. You usually add INCLUDE parameters when the Analysis procedure described in Chapter 6 discloses address space that is unused although occupied.

INCLUDE386=*nnnn-nnnn* (I386)   The same as INCLUDE, but you could put it in a PS/2's MCA.ADL file. It will then serve as an instruction to QEMM386 that would be ignored by the earlier PS/2-specific version of the program, QEMM 50/60.

IOTRAP=*nn*   Sets IOTRAP to *nn*. Use the value 64 for *nn* to have QEMM use an older standard for monitoring I/O port addresses.

LABEL (LB)   Leaves this parameter for OPTIMIZE to use.

LOCKDMA (LD)   Has QEMM let interrupts remain disabled during DMA (direct memory access) transfers; for use with the network software called 10-Net only.

MAPS=*nn* (MA)   Specifies a number of alternate maps for use by DESQview. Each map takes 4K of extended memory. Enter the maximum number of processes you ever run simultaneously under DESQview, plus 1.

MEMORY=*nnnn* (ME, MEM)   Specifies how much raw extended memory QEMM will take charge of, leaving the rest for primitive extended memory users, like the old DOS VDISK. Use a number representing kilobytes from 128 to 32128.

NOCOMPAQFEATURES (NCF)   Disables parameters designed for optimal operation on Compaq PCs, including COMPAQEGAROM, COMPAQHALFROM, and COMPAQ-ROMMEMORY.

NOEMS   Tells QEMM not to act as an Expanded Memory Manager.

NOFILL (NO)   Tells QEMM not to backfill conventional memory to 640K and not to fill video memory. This parameter is useful if your PC has less than 640K of conventional memory and you are using software incompatible with filling, such as Windows enhanced mode.

NOHMA   Tells QEMM that the HMA is already allocated, as in the rare case when you have another memory manager loaded before QEMM that is handling this area.

NOPAUSEONERROR (NOPE)   Tells QEMM not to display the message "Press ESC to unload QEMM or any other key to continue with QEMM" or to allow unloading when it detects an error in a parameter. Use this parameter when the program runs fine despite a technical violation.

NOROM (NR)   Prevents QEMM from remapping the 4K area of the ROM BIOS that contains the routine for rebooting the PC. Try this parameter; if you can reboot successfully, you've saved 4K of extended memory.

NOROMHOLES (NRH)   Tells QEMM not to look for unused areas within blocks of ROM, such as often occur in the ROM BIOS address space, that could be filled with RAM. Such areas may appear unused at boot time but actually be used later, creating conflicts. If this parameter solves something for you, you should run the Analysis procedure, described in Chapter 6, to refine the picture. You can then substitute the appropriate EX-CLUDE parameters for NOROMHOLES and get the greatest use out of your upper address space.

NOSHADOWRAM (NOSH)   Tells QEMM to keeps its hands off shadow RAM created by your system BIOS. Use this parameter if QEMM erroneously detects ROM shadowing where there is none or misidentifies the type in use.

NOSORT (NS)   Tells QEMM not to sort RAM by speed. This parameter is the default in QEMM version 6 and later; it is the opposite of SORT:Y.

NOTOKENRING (NTR)   Tells QEMM not to try to detect a token ring adapter. Use this parameter after QEMM's attempts to detect the board have led to a conflict. You will then also have to explicitly exclude the area used by the token ring board by using an EXCLUDE parameter.

NOTOPMEMORY (NT)   Tells QEMM not to use 384K of memory that is sometimes placed in addresses just below 16MB. Use of this memory sometimes leads to conflicts.

NOVDS   Removes QEMM support for Virtual DMA Services (VDS), a standard for handling communications between a bus-mastering device (such as a SCSI controller) and a memory manager.

NOVIDEOFILL (NV)   Tells QEMM not to extend conventional memory to unused video areas (that is, from A000 to B000 on a monochrome video card or to B800 on a CGA card). This option may resolve conflicts with Windows.

NOXBDA (NX)   Tells QEMM not to move the extended BIOS data area, which is created at 638K or 639K on a few PCs. Otherwise, QEMM will relocate the area to clear the way to extend conventional memory upward. This action will sometimes lead to conflicts with programs that assume the area to be at its usual location.

NOXMS   Takes QEMM out of the business of providing XMS services.

OLDDV (ODV)   Configures QEMM to be compatible with DESQview versions 2.00 and earlier.

PAUSE   Tells QEMM to pause when displaying a message, allowing you to view the message and press Esc to stop QEMM from loading.

RAM or RAM=*nnnn-nnnn*   Tells QEMM to fill available areas of upper memory with RAM for loading resident programs and so forth. If you specify RAM without a value, all available memory is filled. A range of values restricts QEMM to using this range (but you can use the parameter more than once).

REGION (R)   Tells QEMM to relocate part of itself to upper memory region *n* (like the similar LOADHI parameter). This parameter is intended for use by OPTIMIZE. The value 0 tells QEMM to load itself entirely into conventional memory.

ROM, ROM=*nnnn*, or ROM=*nnnn-nnnn*   Tells QEMM to copy contents of ROM at the given address to RAM and then map the RAM to that address in its place. You can give a whole address range, specify a starting address (and assume QEMM can determine the ending address), or use no value to have QEMM replace all ROM in upper memory with RAM.

The ROM parameter allows for execution of BIOS code from RAM, which is faster. It is pointless if your PC's BIOS is already providing ROM shadowing. When you are using Stealth, ROM will act only on 16K blocks; addresses representing a fraction of a block will be ignored.

SORT:Y   Sorts memory by speed, allocating the fastest RAM to conventional memory (where it is usually most heavily used). Consider using this parameter if Manifest Expanded Timings values are faster than First Meg Timings values for conventional memory. This action, however, is incompatible with Windows enhanced mode.

STEALTHROM:*x* (ST)   Enables Stealth. Of the two documented forms of Stealth, set *x* to M to use the mapping method or to F to use the frame method, described in Chapter 5.

SUSPENDRESUME or SUSPENDRESUME:*nn*

(SUS)   Use this parameter if your laptop has the suspend/resume feature. If QEMM issues a message that it can't learn the interrupt used, you will have to provide one as a value. The most likely values are 2, 72, 73, and 77.

TASKS=*nn* (TA)   Sets the number of data structures used to handle interrupts as QEMM switches from protected to real mode. The default number is 16. You would change this number in response to an error message.

UNUSUAL8042 (U8)   Tells QEMM that the PC has a non-standard keyboard controller—a fix to try if running QEMM in the ON state creates keyboard problems.

UNUSUALEXT (UX)   Tells QEMM to use a special method for learning how much raw extended memory is installed. This may enable QEMM to boot when it would not otherwise, but may make the QEMM.COM or Manifest memory reports inaccurate.

VIRTUALHDIRQ:N (VHI:N) Tells QEMM to allow disk caches to perform certain BIOS calls that allow other programs to proceed while the cache is waiting for a read or write from the hard-disk controller, despite the fact that QEMM is using Stealth. QEMM normally defeats this disk cache feature when Stealth is active, because disk caches may corrupt the page frame, upon which Stealth depends. Use this parameter in conjunction with ST if you know that your disk cache preserves the page frame; however, none are known to do so, as of this writing.

VCPISHARE (VS:Y) Tells QEMM to allow VCPI users to share the first page table—not normally advised.

VXDDIR=*d:path* Tells QEMM where WINHIRAM.VXD and WINSTLTH.VXD (used with Windows enhanced mode) are found, if they are not in the QEMM home directory.

VIDRAMEGA (VREGA) Has QEMM make the video RAM region unmappable, equivalent to X-A000-BFFF. This is preparatory to loading VIDRAM (with an EGA or a VGA adapter) and having it annex unused video RAM to conventional memory.

VIDRAMEMS (VREMS) Has QEMM make the video RAM region mappable, but not to fill it with RAM or extend conventional memory into it. This action is preparatory to loading VIDRAM to map RAM from extended memory into this region, to raise the limit of conventional memory.

WATCHDOG=*n* (WD) Has QEMM treat the PC as a PS/2 ($n=1$), a Compaq 386 ($n=2$), or neither ($n=0$) for the purpose of using Watchdog timer features of machines that clone these features, which serve to watch for locked interrupts under DESQview. This parameter won't help you unless you have a machine that has adopted this feature from a PS/2 or a Compaq. (If you have a real PS/2 or Compaq 386, the feature is set automatically.)

LOADHI OPTIONS

LOADHI comprises two programs, LOADHI.SYS and LOAD-HI.COM. LOADHI.SYS commands appear in your CONFIG.SYS file and load device drivers into upper memory. LOADHI.COM commands appear in AUTOEXEC.BAT and load resident programs and Quarterdeck equivalents for DOS resources.

LOADHI.SYS always appears on a line preceded by DEVICE=; LOADHI.COM is invoked by the command LOADHI. Each is followed by any parameters to itself (which begin with a forward slash), then the name of the driver to be loaded or the command for the resident program to be loaded, and finally any parameters to the driver or resident program. Both LOADHI.SYS and LOADHI.COM accept the same parameters.

The most usual way to set up LOADHI commands is simply to run OPTIMIZE and let that program take care of the matter, as described in Chapter 5. There are, however, a number of LOADHI parameters that you can work with yourself to achieve the best fit for your programs. Some of them seem to reflect perennial debates in computer science about the best algorithm for using memory. The big questions are, How do you minimize leftover space, and how do you make allocations most quickly? (Should you take the largest available space, the smallest usable space, or the first usable space, for instance? The answers turn out to be far from obvious.) You can try any method or combination of methods and see which works best for you. The case of letters in these options doesn't matter.

NOTE ⟫

A block *(in the context of using LOADHI) is an available area within a region.*

[No arguments] Lists upper memory areas by region (contiguous space, address range, approximate size, and occupant's name). You typically enter this form of the command at the DOS command prompt.

/?   Lists arguments to LOADHI.

/BESTFIT (/B)   Loads the program into the smallest block into which it fits—a strategy that tends to save larger blocks for larger programs.

/EXCLUDEREGION:*n* (/XR)   Tells LOADHI, in deciding where to load the program, not to consider region *n*.

/EXCLUDELARGEST or /EXCLUDELARGEST:*n* (/XL)   Tells LOADHI, in deciding where to load the program, not to consider the largest region, or the *n*th largest region.

/EXCLUDESMALLEST or /EXCLUDESMALLEST:*n* (/XS)   Tells LOADHI, in deciding where to load the program, not to consider the smallest region, or the *n*th smallest region.

/GETSIZE or /GETSIZE:*filename* (/GS)   Reports how much space the program needs to load and initialize, as well as how much space the program continues to occupy once initialized. If you add an optional file name, LOADHI will write or append the report to that file instead of to the screen.

/HAPPIEST (/H)   Loads the program into the smallest block into which it will fit without terminating with an error code—a refinement on /BESTFIT that will try out blocks until no error is returned.

/HELP   Shows parameters with one-line descriptions.

/LARGEST or /LARGEST:*n* (/L)   Loads the program into the largest available block (or uses the *n* argument to load the program into the *n*th largest available block).

/LINKTOP (/LINK) Connects free upper memory to the DOS memory chain, where it can be allocated to a program running in conventional memory. Try giving the command LOADHI /LINK with no further arguments and then running your DOS application. See if it finds more memory available. Afterward, undo the effect of this command by giving the command LOADHI /UNLINK.

/LO Loads the program into conventional memory. You may find it easier to add this parameter than to remove LOADHI from a command line, for test purposes.

/NOLO (/NL) If the program won't fit into upper memory as specified, tells LOADHI not to load it at all (as opposed to the default fallback option of loading it into conventional memory).

/NOPAUSEONERROR (/NOPE) Tells LOADHI not to pause or generate the message "Press any key to continue, ESC to abort…," even if an error occurs.

/PAUSE Generates the message "Press any key to continue, ESC to abort…" whenever this line is executed.

/REGION:*n* (/R:*n*) Loads the program into region *n*, an area of available space (presumably large enough) within one of the regions listed when you enter LOADHI with no parameters.

/RESIDENTSIZE=*nnnn* (/RES) A parameter passed by OPTIMIZE asserting that the program will need the specified number of bytes when loaded, which LOADHI can compare with the size of the target block.

/RESPONSE or /RESPONSE:*filename* (RF) Looks for the parameters in a response file specified by *filename*, by an environment variable LOADHIDATA, or as the default, LOADHI.REF. Used by OPTIMIZE.

/SIZE:*nnnn* or /SIZE:*nnnn*K   Loads the program into the smallest block larger than *nnnn* bytes or kilobytes, which must be large enough for the program to initialize.

/SMALLEST or /SMALLEST:*n* (/S)   Loads the program into the smallest block or the *n*th smallest block, ignoring its apparent size requirements.

/SQUEEZEF (/SQF)   Uses the page frame to provide additional space to initialize the program. This option makes certain assumptions about the operation of the program and the relative placement of the program and the page frame. Normally used by OPTIMIZE.

/SQUEEZET (/SQT)   Initializes the program in a special temporary memory area (to benefit from the extra room) and then moves it to its permanent location. Normally used by OPTIMIZE.

/TERMINATERESIDENT (/TSR)   Terminates in the manner of a TSR, to satisfy requirements of the INSTALL command in DOS 4.

MANIFEST OPTIONS

You can add parameters to Manifest to make it act as a command-driven program, sending its reports directly to the DOS screen. Use the highlighted letters from the menus that you would type within the program to see a certain screen. For instance, to see the contents of the QEMM-386 Type map screen, enter

```
mft q t
```

Note the space between the letters.

To see the alternate screen (that you would reach from a given screen by pressing F3), add the switch /a. For instance, to see the QEMM-386 Type list screen, enter

mft q t /a

To see all QEMM-386 screens, use an asterisk in place of the second letter, such as

mft q *

You can then redirect this output to a file (by adding >*filename* to the command line) or to a printer (by adding >**lpt1** or your printer port designation).

TIP ⟫

*If there is more than a screenful of output, it will scroll past without interruption. To have Manifest pause and await a key press after each screenful, add the parameter /***p***.*

Manifest also accepts some parameters that affect its starting mode or display as a full-screen, menu-driven program. Note that the case of the letters doesn't matter.

/?   Shows all available parameters.

/A   Shows the alternate screens first (which you otherwise reach by pressing F3).

/B*x*   Looks for CONFIG.SYS and AUTOEXEC.BAT on drive letter *x*. This option might be useful on a network.

/L   Displays 43 lines on an EGA adapter or 50 lines on a VGA adapter.

/M   Displays in two colors—useful on laptop displays that don't interpret color screens well.

/N   Tells Manifest not to suppress snow on a CGA adapter. Try this for a faster display if you have CGA video and no annoying flecks appear when you're running Manifest.

/T   Makes Manifest resident. Even without this parameter, you can make it resident through the Exit menu. Even if you use it, you can unload Manifest (or change the hot-key combination) through the Exit menu.

✗ PART III

GOING

BEYOND

THE LIMITS

WITH

386MAX

THREE ◈

Part III is devoted to 386MAX. In Chapter 8, you will learn how to install the program and maximize use of your upper memory, as well as how to use the shell program MAX and other utilities. Chapter 9 covers how to use the reporting program ASQ to learn about your system and memory, how to resolve conflicting uses of memory, and how to make 386MAX work in a variety of common hardware and software environments. Look to Chapter 10, the 386MAX command reference, to learn how and when to use the various options available with the memory manager and its companion programs.

CHAPTER EIGHT

INTRODUCING

386MAX

X

The Qualitas product 386MAX is a complete memory management package for the PC, featuring a memory manager, installation program, programs for optimizing use of upper memory (which free the greatest possible amount of conventional memory), and programs for system analysis and diagnosis. One program in particular, ASQ, offers extensive information on your system configuration and useful tutorial guidance on its significance to you. It is treated in the next chapter, which also includes some hints for troubleshooting. This chapter will lead you through the process of installing 386MAX and introduce you to the 386MAX utilities, including the shell program MAX, which makes the package's resources available to you through a simple, menu-driven system.

> **NOTE** 〉〉
>
> *The basic product, 386MAX, will run on about any IBM-standard 386 or 486 PC. Qualitas also produces a package just for the IBM PS/2 called BlueMAX, which makes best use of the PS/2 architecture. It otherwise operates much like the product described here.*

INSTALLING 386MAX

Installation is normally a simple process, but the procedure as Qualitas has set it up is vital for expanding files from the distribution disk, conforming 386MAX to your system, and making best use of DOS memory (through the MAXIMIZE program, which you can call from INSTALL). Before you make the installation, note these points:

✗ Make sure that you have about 1.8MB free on your target drive, which should, preferably, be your boot drive and whose data should not have been compressed by a disk compression utility.

✗ Have a bootable floppy disk on hand in case you need it to restart your system, although this is unlikely to be necessary.

✗ If you have device drivers or resident programs that can load themselves into upper memory, configure them to load into conventional memory instead, if possible.

✗ If you want to use Qcache, the Qualitas disk cache, it is easiest to remove existing disk cache commands from CONFIG.SYS and AUTOEXEC.BAT at this time. You can only use one disk cache at a time.

✗ Shorten very long lines that load drivers and TSRs in CON-FIG.SYS and AUTOEXEC.BAT if possible (for example, by adding directories to the DOS PATH rather than by specifying the full path to a command). MAXIMIZE can't handle command lines longer than 128 characters, but it may itself add up to about 60 characters to a line.

✗ While you are editing AUTOEXEC.BAT, add C:\386MAX to your DOS PATH statement (or use your boot drive letter and intended 386MAX directory name). For some reason, the installation program does not perform this service, which will make the MAX utilities more accessible.

✗ Note that Qualitas documentation and program screens refer to conventional memory as "low DOS memory" and to upper memory as "high DOS memory."

Running INSTALL

Simple as the installation process is, something *might* go wrong. Keep in mind these actions you can take to get back to where you started, if need be:

✗ You can exit the program by pressing Esc and following the prompts. INSTALL will restore previous forms of your system files CONFIG.SYS and AUTOEXEC.BAT if need be.

✗ If your system freezes, reboot or reset your computer and, at the beep, press and hold Alt. This action will prevent 386MAX.SYS, the memory manager, from loading, if it has been installed.

✗ If the files have been loaded, make the 386MAX directory current and give the batch file command PREINST, which will restore CONFIG.SYS and AUTOEXEC.BAT from copies that INSTALL has saved.

✗ Look through the troubleshooting hints in Chapter 9 and the 386MAX.SYS parameters in Chapter 10 for the solution for your system.

The installation process itself runs as follows, although the exact sequence may vary with your system configuration:

1. Load the installation disk, and enter **a:install** or **b:install.**

2. Press a key to get past the introductory screen. Press Y if your screen is in color (and if you are asked). Enter the name of your boot drive (press Enter if it appears).

3. Brand your copy with registration information: Enter your name and your serial number (which appears on your registration card and the Rolodex card attached to it). Type no spaces within the serial number.

4. Enter a name for a directory to house 386MAX (or accept the choice offered by pressing Enter). Watch as files are copied.

Note some features of the screen: INSTALL posts its actions in the window at the left, and it offers a "quick reference" on the current stage of the process at the right. You can get help by pressing F1, and, when offered a chance to print a listing, you can do so by pressing F2 and following further prompts.

Help screens have a consistent structure. You can scroll through them with the arrow keys or the arrows near the ends of the scroll bars, and you can page through them with PgUp and

PgDn or the wedge characters at the ends of the scroll bars. You can select other Help areas (shown at the bottom) by highlighting them with Tab and pressing Enter, by pressing the highlighted letter, or by clicking on them with the mouse. Other areas include related topics or a general Help index. Pressing Esc takes you back to the installation screen.

5. Press Y or Enter (equivalent to the highlighted choice), and follow the further prompts if you want Windows 3 support. Press Y to allow INSTALL to modify Windows' SYSTEM.INI file. This adds two lines to the [386Enh] section, VCPIWarning=FALSE and SystemROMBreakPoint= FALSE, described in Chapter 4.

6. Press Y to allow INSTALL to add DOS 5 Help text, and enter your DOS directory path or accept the one shown. This step entails adding some lines about 386MAX programs to the file DOSHELP.HLP, whose contents are shown when you enter **help** with no parameters at the DOS prompt (in DOS 5).

7. Press Y to allow INSTALL to modify CONFIG.SYS, AUTOEXEC.BAT (as well as any batch files that it calls), and the 386MAX profile, found in your 386MAX directory, which contains options to 386MAX.SYS.

8. Press Y if you want to install Qcache, the disk cache, and have removed any lines from your system files invoking other disk caches.

9. Press Y to allow INSTALL to remove or edit lines added or modified by other memory managers. This process will proceed line by line; press Y to approve each change.

TIP

*You can remove the work of other memory managers at any time by entering **stripmgr** at the DOS prompt. You can undo the work of STRIPMGR by running the batch file PRESTRIP.*

10. Press Y to see the changes. Press Esc to return to installation.

11. Press Y to read the README file. Check this file carefully for notes on your hardware and software. You can navigate this file like the Help text described above. Press Esc to return.

12. Press Enter to run MAXIMIZE. If you have another memory manager running, you will be instructed to reboot and will be returned to DOS. Once you've booted, you can start MAXIMIZE as described next.

Running MAXIMIZE

MAXIMIZE is designed to make the most of your DOS memory by filling every available area in upper memory with RAM and then relocating device drivers and resident programs there from conventional memory. Besides running MAXIMIZE as part of the installation process, you should run the program whenever you have added, removed, or reconfigured device drivers, resident programs, or add-on cards that occupy upper memory, because any of these actions can change the optimal configuration. Running MAXIMIZE normally takes only a minute or two.

TIP

Because of the complexity that MAXIMIZE deals with, it may fail or hang somewhere along the line. If it does, exit MAXIMIZE by pressing Esc and following the prompts, if possible. MAXIMIZE will then restore your system files to their former state. If you can't exit, reboot or reset your PC. At the beep, hold down the Alt key to prevent 386MAX from loading, make the 386MAX directory current, and run the batch file PREMAXIM, which will also restore your system files. Try the hints later in this chapter and in Chapter 9, and run MAXIMIZE again.

MAXIMIZE runs in three phases, during which it does the following:

1. Checks for available memory and makes backup copies of your system files.

2. Finds device drivers and resident programs in CONFIG.SYS, AUTOEXEC.BAT, and called batch files (those that have been invoked by the CALL command). It precedes the lines that invoke them with calls to the upper-memory loaders 386LOAD.SYS and 386LOAD.COM, with parameters instructing them to learn the sizes of these programs, both as they initialize and once they are ready to run. In the case of a full maximization, it will give you a chance to review these choices.

3. Learns sizes for drivers and programs as it loads them into conventional memory and then arranges them to load as many as possible into upper memory, making the necessary changes to system files.

After each phase, MAXIMIZE reboots your machine. To start MAXIMIZE from DOS and see the process in detail, make your 386MAX directory current and enter **maximize.** Follow this sequence for Phase 1, which makes preliminary checks and backups:

1. If asked whether your monitor displays in color, press Y or N as appropriate. Read the opening and introductory screens, pressing Enter after each. Enter the name of your boot drive, or press Enter if it appears correctly.

2. Press Y for a quick run of MAXIMIZE or N for a full run, which will allow you to review how MAXIMIZE intends to load drivers and programs. To follow this discussion, you should press N for the fuller form.

3. Press Enter and await a reboot, which is preceded by a pause of a few seconds.

Now you are ready for Phase 2, which identifies programs that are candidates to be loaded into upper memory:

1. A box scrolls up (created by some temporary additions to your AUTOEXEC.BAT file) reminding you that, if your AUTOEXEC.BAT file starts any applications or shell programs, you will have to terminate them to proceed. Press any key, as prompted.

2. Assuming that you chose the full maximization, press Enter for the screen that allows you to view and modify treatment of your drivers and resident programs (Figure 8.1). Here are the essentials of how to navigate this stage:

   ✗ Press F8 to go to the next file (for instance, from CONFIG.SYS to AUTOEXEC.BAT and then to the first batch file called from AUTOEXEC.BAT).

   ✗ Press F7 to return to the previous file.

   ✗ Press ↑ or ↓ to go from line to line.

   ✗ Press F6 to change the action on a line.

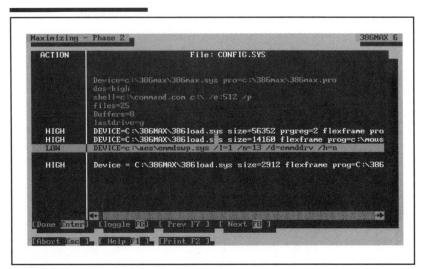

FIGURE 8.1: *The Phase 2 configuration screen*

As to the action, MAXIMIZE will display a value of HIGH if the file is already being loaded into upper memory (as by a previous run of MAXIMIZE), a value of MAXIMIZE to learn the program's sizes (during initialization and after) before loading it into upper memory, or a value of LOW to let it load normally into conventional memory.

3. You can change a value of HIGH to MAXIMIZE or LOW, and you can change a value of MAXIMIZE to LOW, by pressing F6 once or twice. Watch the command line change to reflect the current action:

✗ Change the value from HIGH to MAXIMIZE if you have changed your configuration and you want MAXIMIZE to find a new optimal position for the file.

✗ Change the value from HIGH or MAXIMIZE to LOW if you know that the program won't run in upper memory or must load itself in upper memory. Change the value to LOW if you encountered problems with this program during a previous run of MAXIMIZE. Change the value to LOW if this program has already been called (and loaded into upper memory) earlier in AUTOEXEC.BAT or a called batch file and the present command line only passes some operating values to the program. Finally, change the value to LOW before an internal command used by a command processor other than DOS's COMMAND.COM.

4. When you have reviewed these choices, press Enter until you are clear of these screens.

NOTE ✗

Steps 3 through 7 use the ROMSearch program included in 386MAX and normally run only when you first install the program. You can rerun this procedure at a later time by entering **romsrch** *from the command line. You can then add any lines that are suggested to your 386MAX.PRO file.*

5. MAXIMIZE will search your system for active ROM. With a formatted floppy disk handy, press Y to continue.

6. Nudge your mouse to generate some activity that MAXIMIZE can detect and then press any key.

7. Insert your floppy disk into either drive A or drive B, and press a key.

8. Read the message marking the end of the ROM search, remove the floppy disk, and press any key.

Step 8 normally only appears during your first run of MAXIMIZE and only if you have a VGA adapter. Also, if 386MAX detects the presence of certain specific video chips, it will skip this test.

9. Press Y to agree to load VGAswap, if asked, and press any key. This setting relocates your VGA BIOS into the hole in memory between the VGA graphics and text buffers, leaving a larger contiguous expanse of upper memory available above the video area.

10. Press Enter and observe the reboot into Phase 3.

If you have any problems with ROMSearch or VGAswap, try rebooting your PC; MAXIMIZE should continue from Phase 2. This time, say no to the problem option.

NOTE

You can read tips on getting ROMSearch or VGAswap to work in Chapter 9.

Phase 3 checks sizes of programs chosen as candidates for loading into upper memory, arranges them (as much as possible) in upper memory, writes changes to the system files, reboots the system, and checks the results:

1. Read the note that you saw in Phase 2, about exiting applications, and press any key.

2. Watch as MAXIMIZE checks permutations of program placement and then press any key.

3. MAXIMIZE will display a list of programs that it is loading into upper memory (along with free blocks), as shown in Figure 8.2. Press Enter.

4. Press Enter for the final reboot. As your system is configured now, it should be fully maximized and operational.

As your CONFIG.SYS and AUTOEXEC.BAT files execute now, watch for any error messages or other problems. If you see any, try to identify the offending file. See if you can reconfigure it (for example, by changing parameters so that it doesn't load itself high or use expanded memory). Enter the command PREMAXIM

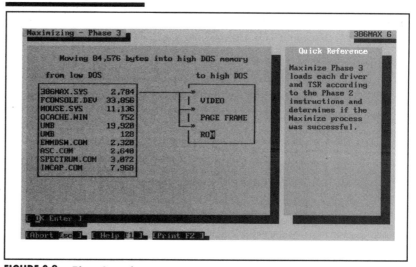

FIGURE 8.2: *Phase 3 results*

and then run MAXIMIZE again. If you were unable to reconfigure the problem command, set its action to LOW on the Phase 3 screen.

> **TIP** ⟫
>
> *If you maintain alternate sets of CONFIG.SYS and AUTOEXEC.BAT files, as suggested at the end of Chapter 3, don't forget to copy your maximized system files back to the appropriate original set.*

USING MAX

MAX is a shell program that gives easy access to the user programs in the 386MAX package: a text editor, the reporting program ASQ, MAXIMIZE, and the quick reporting program 386UTIL. It incorporates the Help system that you have already encountered in MAXIMIZE. Keystrokes and mouse actions that you learn here all apply to ASQ, which we take up in Chapter 9.

Start MAX by entering **max** at the DOS command line. Note these ways you can operate the program:

✗ Choose a major menu item by pressing Alt plus the topic's highlighted letter or by pressing ← or →.

✗ Choose a submenu item by pressing its highlighted letter alone or by pressing ↑ or ↓ and then Enter.

✗ Get help on the current item by pressing F1, or bring up the Help system from the Help menu.

✗ Arrange to print the current item by pressing F2.

✗ Return to the original screen from the Help or Print screen by pressing Esc.

Getting Help with MAX

Bring up MAX Help by pressing F1 from any screen. Here are the essentials:

- ✗ You can scroll through text with ↑ and ↓ or by clicking on the arrows near the ends of the scroll bar.
- ✗ You can page through text using PgUp and PgDn or by clicking on the wedges at the ends of the scroll bar.
- ✗ Note that there are often current topics following the text; on a color screen, their headings appear in red. You can select one by double-clicking on it or by pressing ← or → until it is highlighted and pressing Enter.
- ✗ You can select one of the buttons below the text by double-clicking on it or by highlighting it with Tab or Shift-Tab and pressing Enter. The buttons bring up, from left to right, main Help topics, the Help index, the next in a sequence of topics, and the previous topic. The last button exits Help, as does pressing Esc.

Printing

Print current screen material by pressing F2. You can then choose what to print (the current listing or the related Help topic) and how to print it (to the active printer port, to a new file, or appended to an existing file).

- ✗ Choose a major option by pressing Alt plus the highlighted letter or Tab.
- ✗ Choose a subheading by pressing ↑ or ↓.
- ✗ Activate or deactivate a subheading by pressing the spacebar.

✗ You can choose File Name and type in a new file name. The file will appear in the current working directory unless you include a path.

✗ Press Esc to return to the previous screen.

Using the Editor

MAX includes a handy built-in text editor for modifying your system files CONFIG.SYS and AUTOEXEC.BAT, the 386MAX configuration file 386MAX.PRO, and other text files. It includes some special tricks that are especially handy for adding options to 386MAX.PRO.

You start the editor by choosing one of the first four options on the File menu. Try first, for instance, bringing up your CONFIG.SYS file by pressing Alt-F and C from the main menu. Here are some notes:

✗ The editor comes up in View (read-only) mode. You can scroll through a file as you did Help text. To modify a file, press F6 for Edit. You must then press F7 to save any changes that you have made (or press Y when prompted as you switch away from a changed file).

✗ The editor is initially in Insert mode. To overwrite existing text, first press Ins.

✗ To see a list of navigation keys, press F1 for Help and select Editor Basics. Scroll to near the end of the text.

✗ You can highlight a block of text by pressing Shift plus one or more navigation keys. You can then delete the block by pressing Del or cut and paste the block using other key combinations. Details are under Help Editor Block Operations.

✗ You can add or subtract REM keywords or 386LOAD commands from CONFIG.SYS or AUTOEXEC.BAT with a keystroke. Keys are listed under Editor Special Features.

✗ When you choose to edit the MAX profile and then choose Option (F8), a special editing screen appears, as shown in Figure 8.3. Here, you can add an option before the current line in the profile by highlighting the option (using ↑, ↓, PgUp, or PgDn) and pressing Enter. As you highlight each line, a description appears at the right. These options are also described in Chapter 10.

✗ If there are placeholders (lowercase x, y, or n) appearing in the Options Text box near the bottom of the screen, you must replace them with real values. You can do this either by clicking on the placeholder or by activating the options line (press Alt-T or tab to the line) and moving the cursor into position under the placeholder. Then, press Ins and type in the new value—for example, by typing B000-B8FF in place of $xxxx$-$yyyy$, a placeholder for a range of segment values. You can then press Enter to add the line or Esc to discard the changes.

✗ Press Esc to leave the editor.

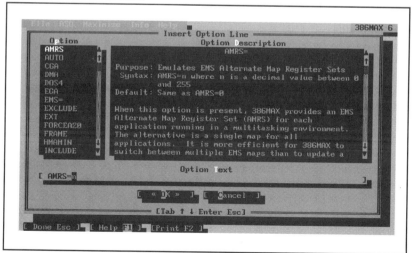

FIGURE 8.3: *Inserting profile options*

Updating 386MAX

You can update your copy of 386MAX using files provided by Qualitas and the Update item on the File menu. Select the item and follow the prompts. You can also run the UPDATE program directly from DOS.

ASQ

The ASQ reporting program is available from the second main-menu entry. You will read more about how to use it in Chapter 9. Note that the last three submenu items here summarize some information provided by ASQ (including memory use, DOS configuration and resource use, and hardware configuration) without actually invoking ASQ.

MAXIMIZE

The third menu item allows you to use the memory optimization program MAXIMIZE. Note that you can choose the full run, which allows you control over how drivers are loaded.

Info

Info submenus call a series of reports produced by 386UTIL.COM, which you can also run from the DOS command line. Table 8.1 shows Info submenu items and their equivalent 386UTIL command-line options.

Exiting MAX

You can leave MAX by pressing Esc or choosing File Exit, and by then pressing Enter when the Exit door appears.

TABLE 8.1: *MAX Info Items and Their Equivalent 386UTIL Options*

INFO SUBMENU ITEM	386UTIL OPTION	FUNCTION
Overview	LIST (/L)	Shows memory allocations
EMS memory	MAPEMS (/E)	Shows EMS users and use
Resident programs	MAPMEM (/M)	Shows resident programs
Device drivers	MAPDEV (/D)	Shows device drivers
Load sizes	SUMMARY (/S)	Shows 386LOAD actions
Memory Scan	RAMSCAN (/R)	Shows memory types and uses
Time memory	TIMEMEM (/T)	Shows memory block speeds

OTHER 386MAX PROGRAMS

Apart from the memory manager and MAX (and the programs that can be called from MAX, directly or indirectly), there are two significant programs in the 386MAX package: Qcache, a disk cache, and 386DISK, a RAM disk.

Qcache

Qcache is a conservative disk cache designed to work reliably with your hard disk under 386MAX. It is a write-through cache, meaning that it sends all writes to disk without delay. This kind of cache cannot work as fast as a write-back cache, which collects write requests and handles them in batches for greatest efficiency. It may be a fallback option if your present, ultrafast cache proves incompatible with 386MAX.

INSTALL will offer to replace Microsoft's SMARTDrive, for instance, if it finds it installed. If you are using SMARTDrive from DOS 5 or Windows 3.0, Qcache will make an excellent replacement. If you are using SMARTDrive from Windows 3.1, however, use that version unless it causes problems.

Qcache is a resident program loaded from AUTOEXEC.BAT, by a line QCACHE (preceded by a path, if needed) followed by parameters. All parameters begin with a forward slash. Qcache parameters are described in Chapter 10.

The all-important size parameter is /S: followed immediately by a decimal number for kilobytes. Important run-time parameters include /F to flush the cache and /P to see current cache parameters.

Put the /F parameter in a batch file you use to reconfigure and reboot your PC; see the end of Chapter 4.

386DISK

The disk driver, 386DISK.SYS, is recommended to create a RAM disk in conjunction with 386MAX. You can create a disk of up to 32MB in size if you have enough RAM. In fact, you can create as many RAM disks as you like by adding more than one invocation of 386DISK to your CONFIG.SYS file.

Load 386DISK by adding this line to CONFIG.SYS:

device=c:\386max\386disk.sys [*size*] [*sectors*] [*entries*] [*type*]

Substitute the drive and directory where your copy of the program is. The parameters are all optional:

✗ For [*size*], put a decimal number representing how many kilobytes you want on your RAM disk. The default is tiny: 64K.

✗ For [*sectors*], use a number for how many bytes each sector on the disk will have. A sector is the smallest whole unit in which disk space can be read or written. (DOS usually works with a pair of sectors, called a cluster.) The default sector size is 128 bytes, but you can use sizes of 256, 512, 1024, or 2048 bytes. Larger sizes make for faster disk access at the price of more disk space wasted. Don't expect the results of changing this parameter to be dramatic.

✗ For [*entries*], substitute how many entries may appear in the root directory of the disk. The default value is 64. If you plan to have more than this number of files on disk, consider organizing them into subdirectories, which you can create through your AUTOEXEC.BAT file.

✗ The [*type*] value determines the kind of memory the disk will occupy. The default value is /XMS for converted extended memory from a memory manager. The other available values—/EMS for expanded memory and /EXT for raw extended memory—will create problems for Windows and other software. They also will generally subvert the functioning of a 386 memory manager like 386MAX, so you should avoid using them if possible.

Now that you have been introduced to 386MAX, Chapter 9 will show you how to use ASQ to study your system's functioning. It will also present some tips and troubleshooting notes.

CHAPTER NINE

WORKING

WITH

386MAX

AND

ASQ

The 386MAX package includes a useful program for studying your system, called ASQ. This chapter tours ASQ and offers some tips for troubleshooting.

USING ASQ

You can start ASQ from the DOS command line (by entering **asq**) or from MAX (by choosing ASQ from the main menu and submenu). Entering **asq /?** from DOS will show you some useful start-up parameters, such as how to run the program in monochrome (use the /B option). As you read about the program in this chapter, try bringing up the screens described and note their contents on your system.

Operate ASQ as you learned to operate MAX in Chapter 8. That is, choose a menu and submenu item, press Enter, read (usually, scroll through) the resulting report, and return to the menu by pressing Esc. As you view a report, you can jump to the next report by pressing F8. This has the effect of returning you to the menu and choosing the next submenu item, or the first submenu item on the next main-menu entry. You can return to the previous item by pressing F7.

Besides the help available when you press F1, ASQ features a tutor that appears when you press F3. It works just like Help, except that it introduces the substantive topic covered by the current report, while Help treats use of ASQ itself.

Using Memory Reports

The heart of ASQ, as far as memory management goes, is the second submenu, Memory. The Memory series of reports will show you the how, what, and where of your memory use.

Summary

Use the summary for a quick look at how conventional, upper, and extended memory are being used, as well as how much expanded memory is allocated or free for use.

You can tell at a glance where your drivers and resident programs are going: whether or not they are being loaded into upper memory. All programs above the 640K mark appear by name with their sizes, in the High DOS (upper memory) listing. Resident programs appear in the Low DOS (conventional memory) listing. Device drivers are lumped into their own category.

Besides programs and ROM listings, the report indicates any available memory in the upper memory area. The High DOS report described later will offer more details.

"Total Physical Memory" shown in this report is conventional memory plus extended memory, not including, for instance, shadow RAM. Extended memory is raw extended memory. Available extended memory is memory unmanaged by 386MAX (perhaps used by a device driver loaded before 386MAX), so it is unavailable to XMS users, such as Windows.

Low DOS

The Low DOS report is a complete record of conventional memory use, including BIOS data (beginning at "interrupts"), file handles and hardware devices (beginning at "IO"), software device-drivers (beginning at "Device Drvrs"—note that, here, device drivers are given by name), DOS resources, DOS stacks, COMMAND.COM, resident programs, and available space. Displayed on the right, you'll see the beginning of the environment (which contains the program's own name, the DOS PATH, and other values) as it has been passed to each resident program. ASQ leaves itself out of the account.

High DOS

You can see at once from the High DOS report shown in Figure 9.1 the effects of the VGASWAP option to 386MAX: Video ROM has been moved from segment C000 to segment B000, leaving a small bit of ROM at C000 and opening memory immediately above that for placing device drivers.

These values bring up the all-important subject of how to interpret address values shown on these screens. Memory addresses are shown in *segment:offset* form, as hexadecimal numbers. You can convert these numbers into their decimal equivalents as shown in Appendix A, or you can just plug the segment numbers straight into option values for the 386MAX.PRO file.

The four digits before the colon are values for a segment register (discussed in Chapter 2). The least significant digit represents jumps of 16 bytes, called paragraphs, through memory; the next digit, 256 bytes; the next digit, 4K; and the highest digit, 64K. Thus, upper memory begins at segment address A000, which is equivalent to an absolute memory address of 640K. Address B000

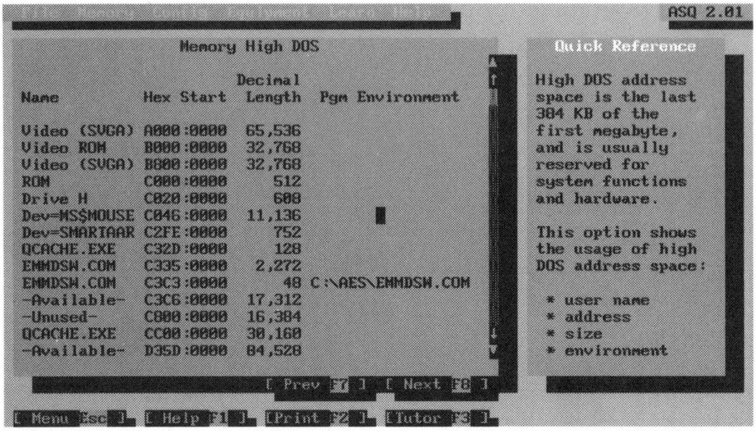

FIGURE 9.1: *The High DOS report*

is 64K higher than that. (The full decimal length is 65,636 bytes, as shown in the figure.) Address B800 is $4K \times 8$, or 32K, higher than B000. The offset (the part of the address shown after the colon) is usually shown as zero, so you can ignore it.

Addresses in 386MAX (unlike in QEMM) end with the first byte beyond the desired range. Thus, if you have a statement USE=F000-F800, you recover a 32K range of memory that actually stops at F7FF. You usually deal with memory in 4K chunks (addresses that end in two zeros).

Look at the Name column in the display—ROM can be real ROM or shadow RAM. RAM mapped by 386MAX appears by the name of the program occupying it or as "-Available-." You can note where available memory falls and consolidate it by positioning your hardware in the address space to make available blocks contiguous. See the instructions for your adapter cards to learn how to relocate their memory.

Addresses marked "-Unused-" are areas ASQ did not identify but where 386MAX has not mapped RAM. You may be able to reclaim some areas like this using the USE parameter to 386MAX (you may be tempted to add USE=C800-CC00 to reclaim the 16K shown), but proceed with caution. In this case, the area marked "-Unused-" starting at C800 is used by a hard-disk BIOS.

ROM Scan

The ROM Scan report, shown in Figure 9.2, lumps upper memory blocks functionally. Thus, all areas filled with RAM are called "HighDOS," whether they are occupied or not. The EMS column conveniently locates the page frame.

Interrupts

Interrupts are events generated by hardware or software that cause the CPU to transfer control immediately from the current

FIGURE 9.2: *The ROM Scan report*

process (the running program) to a routine elsewhere in memory. Interrupts are numbered sequentially according to the events that generate them.

NOTE

You can read more about interrupts in a sidebar in Chapter 6.

The first part of this report shows all the processes that are first in line for one interrupt or another, with their locations in memory and the interrupts they receive. If you scroll down, you reach a serial listing of interrupts with their names and the addresses in memory to which they lead. This list reproduces a table that always occupies the very bottom of DOS memory. If you are an experienced user, you can use this information to learn more about the behavior of programs, such as TSRs.

Extended and Expanded Memory

A series of reports follow on raw extended, EMS, and XMS memory:

✗ The Extended report shows total raw extended memory and how much of it 386MAX has appropriated for all its purposes.

✗ The Expanded report shows figures on EMS use. You can learn from this screen how many handles are available (every EMS application needs at least one), how many are in use, how much memory is allocated to each handle, and how much is allocated all together. You can use this screen to see if you have enough RAM and if enough is available as EMS.

✗ The EMS Usage report shows mappable memory and the page frame in the context of DOS memory as a whole.

✗ The XMS report shows information on the three areas covered by the XMS specification: upper memory, the High Memory Area (HMA), and XMS extended memory. Because 386MAX maintains a single pool of memory, available XMS memory should be roughly equal to available EMS memory unless you have used the EXT or EMS options in the 386MAX.PRO file. (They are described in Chapter 10.)

Access Timing

The Access Timing report shows access times and relative speeds of memory in the DOS address range. The fastest memory in this range is shown with a relative speed of 100 percent; other blocks of memory have speeds shown as a percentage of this.

You can expect blocks of ROM (video ROM, system ROM) to be much slower than RAM, and video RAM will be slower than system RAM. You can print this screen and then convert ROM to RAM by using ROM shadowing or enabling 386MAX's ROM caching. (ROM caching is enabled by default; see the ROM option to 386MAX in Chapter 10.)

If the RAM allocated to conventional memory (below the A000 start address) is not the fastest memory in your system, you may benefit from the SWAP option to 386MAX. See Chapter 10 for further details.

Using Configuration Reports

The Configuration reports show a variety of information recorded in your system, including DOS resources, the DOS environment, the contents of system files, and the values stored in CMOS, the special memory your PC uses to configure itself when you first power up.

✗ The summary shows your DOS version and DOS resources; for instance, you can see at a glance how many file handles and DOS buffers you have available.

✗ Lower on the same screen, you can see a reproduction of your DOS environment, which is simply an area of memory where terms are stored with their values for use by DOS, programs, and users. (For instance, you may be writing batch files that use environment variables.) Common variables are COMSPEC, which tells DOS where on disk to find a good copy of COMMAND.COM, and PATH, which tells COMMAND.COM where to look for programs to execute after you have typed a command. Note the size of the environment—it is set at boot time. If a large part of the environment is not in use, you may be able to reduce its size and save a little conventional memory for your applications. The size is given as a parameter to a line in CONFIG.SYS, which looks something like this for DOS 5:

```
shell=c:\command.com /e:512 /p
```

The number here sets the environment size to 512 bytes. You can substitute a value that suits your needs. If no such line appears, you can add one.

✗ Further menu selections display the contents of your CON-FIG.SYS, AUTOEXEC.BAT, and 386MAX.PRO files.

✗ The last selection shows the contents of your CMOS, which your PC uses to configure itself when it first wakes up, by location and value. These values are raw and may need further interpretation, so you should use them with caution.

Using Equipment Reports

Equipment reports provide you with a record of your hardware configuration and also show some current BIOS settings:

✗ The summary shows the class of PC that you have (the CPU type and speed, for instance), the ROM BIOS maker and version, and installed hardware, including disk drives and parallel and serial ports. This is a handy place to find which revision you have of a particular ROM BIOS. You will sometimes find that you need a BIOS of at least such-and-such a model number and revision date to run a given operating system or environment. ROM BIOS chips are socketed on your motherboard; you can easily substitute replacement chips from your PC's manufacturer.

✗ The Video report shows the type and model of video adapter in your PC, the RAM installed, display dimensions, and the address space the adapter uses.

✗ The Drives report shows floppy and fixed-disk drives installed. You can see at a glance if these values match those of the physical drives; if not, you should run your PC's setup program and check the settings. Note the type shown for your fixed disk, or hard disk: This is the value that must be stored correctly in your PC's CMOS for your hard disk to function correctly. It may also be the hardest value to restore after a CMOS failure (such as when the battery dies). You would do well to note the number on a slip of paper and tape the paper to the back of your PC, for ready reference whenever you have to restore this value.

✗ The Ports report shows I/O address locations for serial and parallel ports. I/O addresses are a scheme of address map separate from the main-memory map addresses occupied by conventional memory and upper memory. To avoid conflicts, each serial and parallel port should normally occupy its own unique address on this map. You can read how to set port addresses in the documentation for your PC or for add-on serial and parallel adapters.

✗ The BIOS detail report shows the contents of the BIOS data area, which is maintained low in conventional memory.

NOTE ⟫⟩

The BIOS report is of interest to advanced users and programmers, who can find a detailed guide to its interpretation in books such as The New Peter Norton Programmer's Guide to the IBM PC & PS/2, *by Peter Norton, Microsoft Press, 1988.*

Using Snapshots

Snapshots (which appear on the File submenu) allow you to save a record of your present configuration for comparisons after you have made changes. You can save a snapshot by choosing File Save and entering a file name (or accepting the default name). Enter a full path if you want the snapshot placed somewhere other than in the current directory. You can later load the snapshot, and then all ASQ screens will reflect the previous configuration rather than the present one.

You may sometimes find it easier to print a report (after pressing F2). You can then have hard copy from a previous configuration as you view a current report, allowing you to compare them side by side.

TROUBLESHOOTING WITH 386MAX

Problems with 386MAX fall mostly under one of three headings: problems involving the MAXIMIZE program, problems with unrecognized uses of upper memory, and other problems involving hardware or software conflicts. This section treats each of these areas.

Solving Problems with MAXIMIZE

Problems with the MAXIMIZE program usually involve using 386LOAD to load programs into upper memory, ROMSearch as it attempts to locate ROM, or VGAswap, which relocates the VGA BIOS. The first step in avoiding these problems is to run MAXIMIZE in full mode and then to eliminate the problem step. Choose the appropriate alternative:

✗ Using the Phase 2 screen, set a problem driver or resident program to load low.

✗ Just say no to VGAswap.

✗ Just say no to ROMSearch.

You may then be able to solve the problem from outside the MAXIMIZE process.

Loading Programs into Upper Memory

If you encounter errors using 386LOAD, try a couple of steps:

✗ Make sure that the programs are not trying to load themselves high: Add a parameter to tell them to load into low memory, if possible.

✗ If the option is available, tell the program not to use EMS memory. Use XMS, if possible.

If you have a driver that you can't make work with 386LOAD, you may find it worthwhile to call Qualitas technical support for further help.

VGAswap

VGAswap is a feature of 386MAX that relocates the 32K VGA BIOS from its normal location at segment C000 to elsewhere (B000 by default). This forms a solid block of video memory beginning at A000 and may create a larger contiguous region of upper memory starting at C000.

If you have hard-disk or other BIOS starting at C800, as is common, note that VGAswap may not make any net difference; you have filled a 32K hole at one location and opened another hole just above it. (You may be able to gain space by relocating the adapter BIOS.) Also, if you use the NOROM option, VGAswap won't take effect, and if you use RAM=, SHADOWROM, or ROM=, any of these may affect its action.

Apart from this, VGAswap may fail if hardware or software tries to use memory starting at B000, or if VGAswap has not read the original video ROM correctly. Here are some fixes worth trying in these cases:

✗ If using VGAswap results in problems with your display using certain software or video modes, try telling it to relocate the BIOS elsewhere. VGAswap (as it appears in 386MAX.PRO) takes optional parameters in this form:

VGASWAP *source segment,target segment,length*

For instance, you could relocate the video BIOS to just below the ROM BIOS by entering the parameters like this:

VGASWAP C000,E800,8000

✗ If you have numerous failures during display actions, try

VGASWAP=C000,B000,8000

to force VGAswap to read the entire BIOS address range. Alternatively, try adding another option

ROM=C000-C800

to achieve the same end.

If this doesn't actually yield more contiguous free upper memory, omit the VGAswap option.

ROMSearch

ROMSearch, which is sometimes performed as part of MAXI-MIZE and which you can also run from the command line, attempts to find further address space to convert to upper memory blocks. It does this by exercising BIOS routines in your PC and looking for addresses that remain uninvolved. At times, this process may conflict with processes on your machine, causing it to lock up. When this happens, you may still be able to use ROMSearch to identify usable address space.

1. Try running the program from the command line by entering **romsrch**. If ROMSearch runs and suggests that you add lines to your 386MAX.PRO file in the form

USE=*nnnn-nnnn*

add them, using a text editor.

2. If the program still fails and you have a PS/2-type mouse, disconnect it and run the program again.

3. If the program still fails, run it again with the parameter /W. See if it displays a line such as

    14: (63/8B)

The first number in parentheses is the number of the interrupt that was being tested when the problem occurred. Reboot and run the program again with the parameter /S followed immediately by the number to tell ROMSearch not to try that interrupt. Be warned that this may make the results of the search less reliable.

Even when ROMSearch runs correctly, its recommendations may be faulty. See the following discussion to see where to pursue your problem next.

Diagnosing Unrecognized Memory Use

Sometimes, adapter cards, such as network cards, will map ROM or RAM into upper memory that can't be detected or sized correctly at boot time. In these cases, 386MAX may map RAM and load programs into an overlapping area, generating conflicts when a program tries to read or write the original memory. Crashes that happen with certain kinds of disk operations or network actions are symptomatic of these conflicts. There are a few useful strategies for curing problems like these.

Study the documentation for network adapters and other cards in your system, and see what addresses they use. Bring up the ASQ Memory High DOS report, and see if any address range occupied by a resident program, a device driver, or the page frame, or else described as "-Available-" overlaps the address range used by the adapter card. In this case, add an option

    RAM=nnnn-nnnn

to your 386MAX.PRO file, where the first offset is the start address for the adapter, and the second is a byte beyond the end address. This will tell 386MAX to leave this region alone. You can include as many such statements as you need. Reboot and run MAXIMIZE to rejuggle the contents of upper memory.

If you can't identify an unrecognized region by studying your documentation, you may have to do some detective work.

ROMSearch appropriates memory more liberally than the memory manager by itself, so its actions are worth attention. Try remarking out USE options in 386MAX.PRO (typically generated by ROMSearch), one by one. Reboot and try to reproduce the problem after each change. You can remove a USE option (or any other option) from effect by preceding it with a semicolon.

Prevent filling of upper memory by adding an option to the end of 386MAX.PRO:

```
RAM=A000-10000
```

Reboot. This will result in many programs being loaded into conventional memory. If it works, however, try excluding only the first half of the area. Edit the option to read

```
RAM=A000-D000
```

Try again. If the problems show up again, try excluding the other half instead. Continue narrowing the range in this fashion until you have nailed down the smallest 4K memory range that avoids the conflict.

You may, conversely, be able to identify usable areas of memory that 386MAX has avoided. Look at ASQ's Memory High DOS report again. If you see areas of ROM that you know are not in normal use (such as hard-disk setup ROM), you can add a line to 386MAX.PRO in the form

```
USE=nnnn-nnnn
```

to allow 386MAX to map RAM to the area.

Solving Hardware and Software Conflicts

A number of hardware and software products pose special problems for 386MAX that can be addressed by special setup options to the product, 386MAX, or both.

> *The README file in your 386MAX directory contains the latest information on correcting various hardware and software conflicts involving 386MAX. Don't neglect to study it. You can solve many problems by scanning the file for information on your system and, in most cases, by adding one or more options to your 386MAX.PRO file.*
>
> *Qualitas also offers several bulletins on solving problems with particular products. You can obtain them through Qualitas technical support or through the online services described at the end of this chapter.*

Problems with Microsoft Windows

The demands that Microsoft Windows places on memory make for a series of sensitive issues involving 386MAX. If you have difficulty running Windows on your system, you should go over the checklist in this section.

Before you concern yourself with how Windows and 386MAX are getting along, you should make sure that Windows is working with the rest of your system. To do this, make up an alternate CONFIG.SYS file using the Windows versions of HIMEM.SYS and EMM386.SYS as your memory manager. (And set up a version of AUTOEXEC.BAT stripped of 386LOAD commands.) You can set up these files like the DOS versions described in Chapter 3.

If you want to use Windows 3.0 in standard mode and 386MAX together, you're out of luck—the combination just isn't supported. Consider upgrading Windows to version 3.1, which works with 386MAX in both standard and enhanced modes.

When you are satisfied that Windows is installed correctly, replace your original CONFIG.SYS and AUTOEXEC.BAT files, and check that the conditions described below are present in your system. They progress from the more basic to the more esoteric. Note that some of the conditions apply to Windows standard mode only; others apply to enhanced mode only. Remember that any changes to your system files or 386MAX.PRO will take effect only after you reboot.

✗ Make sure that you have enough file handles available to Windows. A line in CONFIG.SYS should read FILES=30 or higher. (Either mode)

✗ Make sure that you are leaving Windows at least a mega-byte of XMS memory available beyond what 386MAX is using to fill upper memory, what is being used for a disk cache or a RAM disk, and so forth. (Enhanced mode)

✗ Make sure that there is a file called 386MAX.VXD, which intermediates between 386MAX and Windows protected-mode operation, in your 386MAX directory. If you have 386MAX version 6.0 or later, this should be the file that came with 386MAX, not the one supplied by Windows. If in doubt, reinstall 386MAX to get a clean copy of the file. If you have an earlier version of 386MAX, you should get a new VXD file from one of the Qualitas sources described at the end of this chapter. You should also include the line LOAD=C:\WINDOWS\WINDOWS.LOD, using your path to Windows, in 386MAX.PRO. Better yet, you should update 386MAX to the current version. (Enhanced mode)

✗ Make sure that these lines appear in the section [386Enh] in SYSTEM.INI in your Windows directory:

SystemROMBreakPoint=FALSE

VirtualHighDOS=FALSE

The second line is actually optional. It will allow you to load TSRs into individual DOS sessions under Windows, a 386MAX feature. (Enhanced mode)

✗ Check 386MAX.PRO and remove any instances of the EX-CLUDE option (which limits the EMS swap region, a limitation that Windows can't tolerate) that refer to upper memory. Use the RAM option instead to restrict 386MAX from using an area. (Enhanced mode)

✗ Remove an option that reads EMS=0 from 386MAX.PRO, if you find it there. (Standard mode)

✗ You can't backfill conventional memory and then use enhanced mode, which doesn't recognize the way that the memory manager remaps memory in this case. If you have less than 640K on your motherboard, add the NOLOW option to 386MAX.PRO to prevent backfilling. Likewise, try removing the SWAP option if it now appears. (Enhanced mode)

✗ Try removing the VGASWAP parameter from 386MAX.PRO to fix strange screen behavior. (Either mode)

✗ You may be able to fix certain problems with video drivers by adding the option RAM=C000-C800 to 386MAX.PRO, to keep 386MAX out of this video area. Beyond that, try to obtain a current video driver—one made for Windows 3.1 —from the maker of your video adapter. (Either mode)

✗ Try the procedure described in the earlier section "Diagnosing Unrecognized Memory Use" to identify areas in upper memory where 386MAX or Windows or both may be coming into conflict with adapter memory. Add RAM= statements to 386MAX.PRO to cover these areas; they will exclude both 386MAX and Windows from using them. (Either mode)

✗ Try avoiding conflicts over the monochrome video area by commenting out (placing a semicolon before) a line in 386MAX.PRO that may read USE=B000-B800. (Either mode)

✗ Check the location of the page frame—you can easily locate it on the ASQ Memory Low DOS or High DOS screen. If the page frame appears in conventional memory (below segment address A000), make space for it available in upper memory—for instance, by unloading one or more resident programs—then rerun MAXIMIZE. (Either mode)

✗ Look for any device drivers or resident programs (especially disk caches or RAM disks) that are configured to use expanded memory. Reconfigure them (change their options) to use XMS if possible; otherwise, consider replacing them. (Either mode)

✗ If you use a bus-mastering disk controller (most likely a SCSI controller), make sure that your disk cache is configured to provide double buffering or that you have the proper VDS driver from the drive manufacturer. (See Chapter 4.) You should be able to use Qcache with these drives without special options, because it provides double buffering by default. (Either mode)

✗ Double-check that you are not loading both SMARTDrive and Qcache. (Either mode)

Using DR DOS

386MAX works with DR DOS version 6 once you take a few special steps during the installation process:

1. Remove a line from CONFIG.SYS that reads

```
?"Load memoryMAX software (Y/N)"
```

2. Add a line

   DEVICE=C:\DRDOS\HIDOS.SYS /bdos=ffff

3. Run 386MAX INSTALL, but don't choose to run MAXIMIZE.

4. Make sure that the line that loads HIDOS.SYS in CON-FIG.SYS comes right after the line that loads 386MAX.SYS. (Move it there if necessary.) The 386MAX.SYS line in turn should follow a line that reads HIDOS=ON.

5. If lines occur that load SSTORDRV.SYS and DEVSWAP.COM, move them to precede HIDOS=ON.

6. Reboot and run MAXIMIZE as usual.

Using Disk Compression Utilities

Installing and using 386MAX on a system using disk compression utilities like Stacker and SuperStor can be fairly intricate. You should obtain one of Qualitas's technical notes named STACK.TXT and SUPER.TXT, and follow the procedures described exactly. You can find the technical notes through one of the sources described in the last section of this chapter. A hint: Life with disk compression is much simpler if you leave drive C as your boot drive (don't swap it with another drive), leave it uncompressed, and install 386MAX on it.

Problems with Floppy Drives

Most problems with floppy-disk drives (not-ready errors, data errors) happen when 386MAX maps timing-sensitive ROM code into much faster RAM. The cure is to leave the code in ROM.

Try adding the option NOROM to 386MAX.PRO. If this works, you can narrow the area of ROM affected: Look at the ASQ Memory ROM Scan report. Remove the NOROM option from 386MAX.PRO, and add RAM= options for each area assigned to ROM instead. If the drive still works, remove RAM= options until the problem reoccurs, and then add the last option back. You can try narrowing the scope of the remaining RAM= option until it covers just one 4K block of upper memory.

If this approach doesn't work, try setting a RAM= option to cover a 32K block of upper memory, starting with RAM=C000-C800, and then change it to RAM=C800-D000 and so on, up to RAM=D800-E000. When one of these options works, try narrowing it to cover only the first half of the area—for instance, RAM=C000-C400. Try narrowing the area to a single 4K block.

If this approach doesn't work, try adding a NOWARMBOOT option, and then try commenting out any USE options in effect, one by one.

If this doesn't work either, try the DMA option—for instance, DMA=128. If it works, see if you can use a smaller value. Also, add an option to the line that calls your disk cache to tell it not to cache the floppy in question. (For instance, put **-A -B** on the SMARTDRV command line to tell SMARTDrive not to cache your floppy drives.)

Finally, try not loading TSRs, one by one, to see if one of them is causing a conflict.

Keyboard Problems

Keyboard problems typically manifest themselves as missed keystrokes and apparently stuck keys. When the delay 386MAX creates as it must switch from protected mode to real mode and back to handle a keystroke (added on to delays that your TSRs and applications are already creating) becomes longer than the time between incoming keystrokes, later keystrokes are missed.

To begin solving this problem, try adding an option RAM= F000-10000 to 386MAX.PRO to prevent 386MAX from transferring your ROM BIOS into RAM. If this works, try narrowing the problem by specifying only the first half of the area (RAM=F000-F800) and reboot. Continue dividing and narrowing the problem until you have it localized in a 4K area of memory. You can also simply try the option NOWARMBOOT.

Alternatively, try removing your TSRs one by one and see if removing any one TSR solves the problem.

Computer Hangs at Boot

A variety of conflicts, mostly in upper memory, could cause 386MAX to hang your PC. Try these fixes to see if one of them solves the problem. Remember that you can boot without 386MAX (and bypass the lockup) by pressing and holding Alt at the beep and then pressing a key as prompted. This will give you a chance to edit your configuration files.

✗ Try NOXRAM to keep 386MAX from trying to recover shadow RAM. This might work if your PC's BIOS is doing ROM shadowing in a way that 386MAX doesn't recognize. Alternatively, try turning off your PC's ROM shadowing through its setup program, and let 386MAX do the job of replacing ROM with RAM.

✗ Try NOROM to keep 386MAX from mapping RAM in place of ROM. If this works, try using the RAM option instead. Progressively narrow the area covered, as described in the section "Problems with Floppy Drives" above.

✗ Try certain options to prevent 386MAX from filling memory on nonstandard video systems: Add the option VGA or EGA, as appropriate to your system. Remove any of these options: MONO, CGA, VIDMEM=MONO, or VIDMEM=CGA.

Mouse Problems

Mouse problems are as varied as mouse drivers. Here are a few frequently useful fixes:

✗ Get the latest driver for your mouse from the maker. If the mouse maker maintains a CompuServe forum, you may find the latest driver there.

✗ Put the mouse on COM1 or COM2 instead of COM3 or COM4, if it is a serial mouse. Make sure to move any serial device that is using COM1 or COM2 elsewhere, and to adjust program settings to reflect the changes.

✗ Try not loading the mouse driver in upper memory.

✗ If you are using a driver called MOUSE.SYS, try substituting MOUSE.COM, and vice versa.

Network Problems

Most network problems result from 386MAX not recognizing ROM or RAM used by the adapter. See the earlier section "Diagnosing Unrecognized Memory Use" for techniques to locate the problem address area. The Qualitas technical note NETWORK.TXT, which you can obtain through the sources described at the end of this chapter, has more information on some specific brands of network.

Privileged Operation Exceptions

Privileged Operation Exceptions are the results of software bugs that may never surface until you run your system in protected or V86 mode under a memory manager, which is in a position to spot illegal operations on memory. Often, these problems can be caused by a resident program or an interaction between two resident programs.

Try these techniques for dealing with them:

✗ Try changing the load order of resident programs, that is, the order of the lines that load them in AUTOEXEC.BAT.

✗ Try telling MAXIMIZE to load one or more of them low, in conventional memory.

✗ Try removing one or more of them.

✗ Try searching for RAM or ROM that 386MAX may be mapping over, using techniques in the earlier section "Diagnosing Unrecognized Memory Use."

Video Problems

Problems can arise from conflicts between 386MAX and various nonstandard video adapters over the video address range in upper memory. Here are a couple of possible quick fixes:

✗ Remove any USE options from 386MAX.PRO that apply to video addresses (typically segments A000-C800 but sometimes extending to D000).

✗ Add the option EGA or VGA, as appropriate to your adapter.

Qualitas's technical note VIDEO.TXT lists special options for a number of brands and types of video adapter.

"Packed File Corrupt" Errors

"Packed File Corrupt" errors result from a bug in some applications that surfaces when the applications are loaded in the bottom 64K of conventional memory—a result of your success in transplanting DOS and other programs to the High Memory Area or to upper memory. To avoid these errors, preface calls to problem programs with the DOS 5 command LOADFIX.

FOR FURTHER ASSISTANCE...

You can get technical support, technical notes, patch files, and other material for 386MAX through at least two online sources. Each is a pleasant and productive alternative to a morning spent listening to hot-tub music over a long-distance phone connection.

The Qualitas Bulletin Board

You can reach the Qualitas bulletin board directly by dialing 301-907-8030, or try 301-907-8035 for a 9600-bps connection. Set your communications program to the usual bulletin board settings: 8 data bits and no parity. The ANSI BBS terminal emulation is ideal, and ZMODEM and other common file-transfer protocols are available.

Sign on as prompted. Note that you can make the fullest use of the board after you have registered, that is, after you have left a note for the system operator containing the Qualitas product name and your serial number. Press C at the main menu to initiate the registration process.

You can read more about using communications software and bulletin boards in my books *Up & Running with PROCOMM PLUS 2.0* (SYBEX, 1991) and *Understanding PROCOMM PLUS 2.0* (SYBEX, 1991).

CompuServe

Qualitas currently occupies a section on a CompuServe PC vendor forum, which you reach by entering **go pcvena** at a CompuServe command prompt. You can then choose Section 8 under Messages/Select or Files to find Qualitas material. You can also find coverage of memory management in forums devoted to your favorite environments and applications; for instance, take a look at the Memory Issues section of the Windows Advanced Forum, which you reach by entering **go winadv**.

My book *Up & Running with CompuServe* (SYBEX, 1991) covers all the essentials for joining CompuServe and using its forums.

Now that you are aware of general approaches to working with 386MAX, you should peruse the command reference in the next chapter to see what further options may aid the operation of your system. Besides covering options to the memory manager proper, Chapter 10 details how to limit availability of certain kinds of memory and includes a full set of options to Qcache, Qualitas's disk cache.

CHAPTER TEN

386MAX

COMMAND

REFERENCE

X

Memory management programs have numerous options to adapt their operation to various systems and software configurations. Sometimes your best approach to resolving a problem is to search through the options, find one that seems to meet your needs, and try it. This chapter covers options to the 386MAX memory manager itself, 386MAX.SYS, as well as to the program that controls its operation, 386MAX.COM, and the programs responsible for loading other programs into upper memory, 386LOAD.SYS and 386LOAD.COM. It also covers options to the Qualitas disk cache, QCACHE.EXE, and to a program that limits allocation of raw extended memory, MEMLIMIT.EXE.

386MAX.SYS OPTIONS

Options to 386MAX.SYS are collectively known as your system profile and normally go into 386MAX.PRO, an ASCII file kept in your 386MAX directory. Each option goes on a line by itself. As with all 386MAX options, case of letters does not matter. Some options are created automatically by INSTALL and MAXIMIZE. You can add or remove options using either the MAX editor (described in Chapter 8) or any other text editor. To "comment out," or remove an option from effect, for test purposes, precede the option with a semicolon.

You can also place an option as a parameter on the 386MAX. SYS line in CONFIG.SYS. This is sometimes a convenient choice for testing an option in a given setup.

In the examples that follow, a four-letter placeholder *nnnn* stands for a hexadecimal segment address that you can obtain from an ASQ Memory report or from some other source, such as program or hardware documentation. Start and stop values normally end in two zeros to represent a multiple of 4K. (386MAX stop values are actually one greater than the last byte affected.) A placeholder with fewer characters (such as *n*) represents a *decimal* number, which you provide as described in the entry.

AMRS=*n* Creates EMS alternate map register sets for expanded memory users under multitasking environments, notably DESQview (but not Windows). These sets speed up switching between processes by preserving the register values for each program in memory. They exact a small cost in extended memory. For best performance, set *n* to a number at least one greater than the maximum number of programs you ever run under DESQview simultaneously. The default value is 0, which creates no alternate maps.

AUTO, ON, OFF This set of options is simpler to use than it seems. 386MAX is normally set to ON. Add the option AUTO to prevent 386MAX from backfilling conventional memory or filling upper memory with RAM, when these actions lead to compatibility problems. You can substitute the option OFF to turn off EMS and XMS support, remapping of ROMs, and Weitek math coprocessor support as well. This may allow you to run a protected-mode program that doesn't abide by the VCPI standard. You can use these values as command-line options to 386MAX.COM; see the section that follows for more information.

CGA This option allows 386MAX to fill some address space unused by a CGA (Color/Graphics Adapter) video adapter with RAM and append the space to conventional memory, extending it to 736K. Add the option if you have a CGA adapter and 386MAX has not already performed this action for you, as you can see from the ASQ Memory summary. Test the option thoroughly for compatibility with your software.

DMA=*n* 386MAX sets the DMA (direct memory access) buffer to 16K, or else to 64K if the hard-disk controller uses DMA. You can set this value manually to any value from 8 to 128, representing kilobytes. Set this value higher than the default if you receive an error message from some program indicating that you need a larger buffer.

DOS4   Add this option if you use DOS version 4 and use the /X switch on the BUFFERS line in CONFIG.SYS to load buffers into expanded memory. A better choice would be to remove the /X switch. The best choice would be to upgrade to DOS 5.

EGA   Tells 386MAX not to extend conventional memory into EGA (Enhanced Graphics Adapter) memory space. The switch is used when 386MAX has failed to recognize an EGA adapter. If you see bizarre video effects or find that your system hangs when running in an EGA graphics mode, try adding this option.

EXCLUDE=*nnnn-nnnn*   Tells 386MAX not to make region *nnnn-nnnn* mappable. Try this option if you have problems with an application that uses EMS. The start and stop addresses may range from 1000 (64K) to A000 (640K), except that they may extend to B000 for a monochrome adapter or to B800 for a CGA adapter. It may be simplest to exclude the whole range of mappable conventional memory, from 1000 to A000 (or to B000 or B800). Always specify numbers with the second digit 0, 4, 8, or C ending in two zeros, which have the effect of starting and stopping at 16K boundaries, a requirement for EMS-related addresses.

FORCEA20   Has 386MAX virtualize the A20 CPU line, which controls the High Memory Area. Try this option if your machine hangs, and if you can trace the problem to a program that controls this line. Such programs are usually machine-specific setup utilities.

FRAME=*nnnn*   Tells 386MAX where to locate the page frame, which it usually places automatically. Use this option if the current location is a problem and if you can create space at a new location. (For example, if the usual location at E000 is too high for some programs, you could set it to D000).

HMAMIN=n Tells 386MAX not to allow a program to use the High Memory Area unless that program requests at least n kilobytes. The option might occasionally be useful if your programs include a number of potential HMA users (since only one can actually be assigned the area). You can start n at 64 and work down until a program actually loads into the HMA (as shown by ASQ's Memory XMS report). This ensures that only a program that would use a substantial part of the HMA gets the chance. Most users, however, will use a DOS=HIGH statement to reserve the HMA for the DOS kernel and buffers, making this option moot.

INCLUDE=$nnnn$-$nnnn$ **or INCLUDE=**n Adds to the default mappable memory used for EMS swapping, by subtracting from upper memory blocks available to load device drivers and resident programs. Some programs (such as some versions of Paradox) will use mappable EMS memory (which is distinct from the page frame) to swap code into the 1MB DOS address space. The default mappable area extends from 64K to 640K in conventional memory. You can tell 386MAX to devote n additional 16K pages to the swapping region, letting it choose the addresses, or you can specify a segment address range to include. Use areas that ASQ lists as available, or use additional video-memory addresses gained through the CGA and MONO options. (See these entries for details.) If you have multiple areas to include, add several instances of this option.

MONO   If you have a monochrome adapter (and 386MAX has not already identified it and performed the action), you can use this option to tell 386MAX to fill unused address space at the bottom of video memory and add it to conventional memory, bringing the conventional memory total up to 704K.

NOCOMPROM   386MAX will normally compress the ROM BIOS on some Compaq and Compaq-clone PCs, yielding up to 32K additional upper memory. If you have trouble using floppy drives in such a machine, try adding this option to suppress ROM compression.

NOFRAME   Tells 386MAX not to create an EMS page frame but to support EMS otherwise. Lotus 1-2-3 version 3.0 and some other VCPI clients will work with this feature, which will save you 64K of DOS memory.

NOHIGH   Tells 386MAX not to fill upper memory with RAM. Using this option is often an initial troubleshooting step to see if upper memory filling is conflicting with unidentified adapter memory. If using this option solves your problem, you can then replace it with one or more RAM= options pinpointing the contested areas, as described in Chapter 9.

NOLOADHI   Tells 386MAX.SYS not to load about 4K of itself into upper memory but to load completely into conventional memory. Use this option for troubleshooting or to leave just enough contiguous upper memory to hold a large driver or resident program. (Before using this option, use ASQ Memory High DOS to see where 386MAX.SYS is being loaded and how much available memory adjoins it.)

NOLOW   Tells 386MAX not to backfill conventional memory to 640K (or higher, in systems with monochrome or CGA adapters), when your motherboard has less than 640K. Use this option when you have less than 640K of main memory and backfilling conflicts with software, as it does with Windows enhanced mode.

NOROM   Tells 386MAX not to substitute RAM for ROM. Normally, the manager will try to detect ROMs in upper memory, copy the instructions to RAM, and map the RAM into the original locations. Use this option when the ROM code works only when executed slowly, as floppy-disk ROM sometimes does. If this option solves your problem, try removing it and substituting a RAM= option for different areas of ROM memory (as shown in the ASQ Memory ROM Scan report) until you find the exact 4K address space. In this way, you preserve the speed benefits of mapping ROM to RAM elsewhere. Alternatively, use the ROM= option to limit this action to one or more areas.

NOSCSI Tells 386MAX not to test your system for a SCSI (small computer system interface) device. Try this option if your system hangs as the memory manager is initializing, whether or not you have a SCSI device.

NOWARMBOOT Tells 386MAX not to remap the ROM BIOS area that contains the routine for warm boots. Normally, 386MAX monitors this area so that it can perform a shutdown. If you have trouble booting your PC, try adding this option.

NOWIN3 Removes 386MAX support for Windows 3. Add this option if you don't use Windows 3, to gain about a kilobyte of conventional memory otherwise used by support routines.

NOXBIOS The extended BIOS data area is created by some microchannel, Compaq, and Hewlett-Packard machines at 638K or 639K in conventional memory. Since it gets in the way of extending conventional memory using the MONO, CGA, or VGAswap option, 386MAX normally relocates the XBDA (also called the XBIOS), if it finds it, lower in conventional memory, below where programs are loaded (but see also the XBIOSHI option). If you have programs that assume that the XBIOS is in its original location, add this parameter. Typically, conflicts occur with SCSI controller code and appear as hard-disk access problems.

NOXRAM Tells 386MAX not to reclaim leftover shadow RAM in your system, as it will try to do when it detects one of several Chips and Technologies chip sets. Try this option if your system hangs as the memory manager loads. The effect of this option is the opposite of SHADOWRAM.

PRGREG=*n* Available upper memory blocks (UMBs) are numbered from lower addresses to higher addresses, starting from 1 and going up to 9. This option specifies a region for 386MAX.SYS to load itself. The value 0 tells it to load into conventional memory. This option is usually added by MAXIMIZE.

PRO=*path* Tells 386MAX.SYS where you keep its profile 386MAX.PRO, if not in a directory named 386MAX on your boot drive. Obviously, this option goes not in 386MAX.PRO but in CONFIG.SYS, as a parameter on the line that loads 386MAX.SYS.

PSMEM=*n* **or PSMEM=***n,nnnn* This option is set up for use with a debugger, a programming tool, called Periscope. Qualitas and the makers of Periscope have evolved a joint specification, called the Qualitas/Periscope Memory Management Specification (QPMS), and this option enables 386MAX to conform to it. Add the option with *n* set to how much extended memory to give Periscope, and *nnnn* set to an address in upper memory for the debugger itself to occupy. See your Periscope documentation for further details.

RAM=*nnnn-nnnn* Specifies an area of upper memory that 386MAX will not map over. This option is used to specify occupied address spaces (whether RAM or ROM) that 386MAX has failed to identify automatically, typically because they were not used at start-up or the lengths of ROMs were specified incorrectly by the ROM code itself. Specify start and end addresses at multiples of 4K in DOS memory, that is, segment addresses that end in at least two zeros. The end address is actually the first byte of the next higher block. You can learn these addresses by applying techniques described in Chapter 9.

You can use multiple address spaces on one line by separating them with commas. You can also include more than one line with the RAM option in your profile 386MAX.PRO.

ROM=*nnnn-nnnn* Specifies a block of ROM in upper memory for 386MAX to fill with RAM, after copying the original ROM instructions into RAM. Using this option turns off the default action, which maps all identified ROM to RAM in this fashion; use it when you want 386MAX to be selective. (See the NOROM option for further suggestions.) You can identify areas of ROM using the ASQ Memory ROM Scan report.

You can use multiple address spaces on one line by separating them with commas. You can also include more than one line by using the ROM option in your profile 386MAX.PRO.

SHADOWRAM If your system has shadow RAM provided by one of certain Chips and Technologies chip sets or clones, 386MAX may be able to reclaim leftover shadow RAM to add to its memory pool. Try adding this option and see if available memory (as reported by, for instance, Total EMS+XMS Memory in the ASQ Memory Summary) increases by about 200K. If it doesn't, 386MAX may have already detected the chip set and reclaimed the memory by default. See also the option with the opposite effect, NOXRAM.

SHADOWROM When your system would, absent 386MAX, remap video ROM to a new address (typically from C000 to E000), this option tells 386MAX to allow this original system function. Normally, 386MAX blocks this action, remaps the ROM to RAM, and relocates the RAM itself (using VGAswap) to minimize or eliminate memory fragmentation. This option prevents these 386MAX interventions and is used when they lead to conflicts.

SWAP=*n* If your motherboard memory is slower than your extended memory (as sometimes happens when you have a 386 accelerator card), you may find this option helpful, or 386MAX may be supplying its action by default. Look at the ASQ Memory Access Timing report and see if any memory below A000 is slower than upper memory blocks that have been remapped from extended memory. If so, try adding SWAP= followed by the decimal number of kilobytes needed to replace the slow memory, or that you can spare from extended memory, up to 640. The number should be a multiple of 4. Remove the option, or try specifying SWAP=0, if you have problems with Windows enhanced mode.

SYS=*name* Identifies your system to 386MAX. This option is currently needed only for the Intel Inboard 386 accelerator (for which *name*=INBOARD) and the Orchid Jet 386 (for which *name*=JET386).

TOP384 Recovers top memory, which is 384K of memory just below 16MB that is specially allocated on Compaq PCs and clones. 386MAX will perform this action itself on Compaqs; if you have a Compaq clone, add this option and see if your available memory, reported as Total EMS+XMS Memory in the ASQ Memory Summary report, increases by this amount.

USE=*nnnn-nnnn* Tells 386MAX to fill a block of upper memory with RAM that it would otherwise leave alone. You can specify, for instance, USE=B000-B800 to allow 386MAX to fill EGA or VGA video memory unused with color displays (using VGAswap with the default target address, however, preempts this action). You can also add USE statements if you can identify blocks of BIOS that are unused in normal operation, such as setup routines. On the other hand, you may have to remove USE options, whether you determined them or MAXIMIZE added them as a result of a ROMSearch, if their use conflicts with existing ROM or with software seeking to use an area. You can read more about this in the section called "Troubleshooting with 386MAX" in Chapter 9.

Specify start and end addresses at multiples of 4K in DOS memory, that is, segment addresses that end in at least two zeros. You can use multiple address spaces on one line by separating them with commas. You can also include more than one line by using the RAM option in your profile 386MAX.PRO.

VGA   Keeps 386MAX from adding the VGA video buffer address space to conventional memory, when 386MAX has failed to identify a VGA adapter. Add this option if you see garbage on the screen or your system crashes in VGA graphics modes, or perhaps when your ASQ Equipment Summary report doesn't reflect the presence of a VGA or SVGA adapter.

VGASWAP or VGASWAP=*nnnn,nnnn,n* Tells 386-MAX to move your VGA BIOS to a new location in upper memory, which may make a larger contiguous block of upper memory available and enable relocating a larger resident program from conventional memory to upper memory. This option additionally transfers the code from ROM to RAM, to improve speed. Allow MAXIMIZE to add the VGASWAP option, or add it yourself if you see that moving VGA BIOS from the C000-C800 range would make more contiguous upper memory available, as reflected in the ASQ Memory High DOS report.

✗ Add the optional first parameter if your original VGA BIOS does not begin at C000. Specify the segment value of the actual beginning address as you find it in the ASQ Memory High DOS or Equipment Video report.

✗ Add a segment address as the optional second parameter, after a comma, if you want to relocate the BIOS somewhere other than B000. Choose an address at the beginning of a 32K area of available upper memory.

✗ Add a decimal number (normally 32) as the third parameter (the two commas must precede it) if 386MAX does not recognize the full length of your video BIOS without your help (if, after you first try this option, ASQ Equipment Video does not report the full address range of your relocated BIOS).

If you have a USE= option that overlaps one of the areas that you specify for VGASWAP, VGASWAP will take precedence. Try removing VGASWAP if hang-ups or other conflicts occur as a result of video display actions. See Chapter 9 for more information on use of this option.

VIDMEM=*nnnn-nnnn* Use this option when 386MAX's appropriation of video RAM address space on your system has created problems, either because it has misidentified your video card or because other software has contrary expectations of this address area. It tells 386MAX to leave the area alone. For monochrome adapters, use the address range B000-C000; for CGA, use B800-C000; for EGA and VGA, use A000-C000.

VXD=*path* Add this option when the file 386MAX.VXD is located somewhere other than in the 386MAX directory on your boot drive, to enable necessary support for Windows enhanced mode.

WEITEK=ON, OFF, FORCE You can set this option to ON or OFF to turn support for a Weitek math coprocessor on or off, either by including the option in your profile 386MAX.PRO or by entering 386MAX followed by the option and a value at the command line. If you see a message saying that 386MAX cannot detect a Weitek processor (but you know that one is installed and working), use the value FORCE instead of ON.

XBIOSHI Tells 386MAX to move an extended BIOS data area (if your machine has one) from its original location at 638K or 639K to a new position in upper memory, thus freeing 1K or so of conventional memory. The default option moves the area lower in conventional memory. Either of these actions enables 386MAX to raise the conventional memory limit, provided that your video adapter can part with memory above 640K. Both

XBIOSHI and the default action may conflict with certain software. To have 386MAX leave the XBDA alone, use NOXBIOS.

XMSHNDL=n   Has 386MAX make available the given number of handles for programs that use XMS memory. The default number of handles is 32, but you can set n to anything from 2 to 65535. Each handle takes up six bytes of extended memory. You can set the number to leave a few EMB handles available, as shown in ASQ's Memory XMS report, when you have loaded all the applications that you normally run at a time.

386MAX.COM OPTIONS

You can enter 386MAX at the DOS command line, followed by one of these options, to control or report on some actions of the memory manager or of your system. The case of the letters does not matter.

AUTO, OFF, ON   Puts the system into (ON) or out of (OFF) virtual 86 mode, or allows 386MAX to enter or leave this mode whenever a program requests EMS functions (AUTO). Several common 386MAX settings, however, force the system into V86 mode regardless of this setting; see AUTO under 386MAX.SYS settings for more information.

LIST   Shows a map of DOS memory (the first megabyte), a display of how much upper memory (called HIGH memory) is available and the largest free block size, a summary of how raw extended memory is being used, and the current state of the system (whether ON or OFF).

LOADHIGH and LOADLOW   To load programs into upper memory, give the command 386MAX LOADHIGH, one or more commands to load TSRs, and the command 386MAX LOADLOW. This method is rarely used.

MAPEMS   Displays a list of EMS handles and the amounts of memory allocated to each, along with a map of DOS memory showing mappable memory and the page frame.

MAPMEM   Displays a list of allocations of DOS memory, by name of owner—that is, the program that was allocated the memory—start and stop addresses, start address of the owner, total length, and interrupts the program is first to receive (in the case of program areas) or the first few characters of the environment (in the case of environments).

RAMSCAN   Displays a list of conventional memory size, upper memory by type and address range ("High DOS memory" is upper memory filled with RAM), and extended memory by type of use and handle. Also displays summaries of upper memory ("High DOS address space") and extended memory use.

TIMEMEM   Displays access times and relative speeds for blocks of memory in your system. Blocks are identified by absolute start addresses, address ranges in decimal kilobytes, and lengths.

WEITEK=ON, OFF   Turns support on and off for a Weitek math coprocessor in your system. See the section on 386MAX.SYS for more information.

386LOAD OPTIONS

The list of options in this section is mostly for your information, since these options are, for the most part, used as needed by MAXIMIZE. You may find some options useful for debugging, for tinkering with program placement in upper memory, or for dealing with special requirements of certain resident programs.

The term *regions*, as used here, refers to successive blocks of available upper memory, with Region 1 being the lowest. Regions may thus be numbered 1 through 9. Options are common to 386LOAD.SYS and 386LOAD.COM except as noted. The last option is always PROG=, and it is followed by the name of the program to load, preceded by its path, if necessary, and followed by parameters to the program. Changes to these options take effect after you have rebooted your system.

DISPLAY Has 386LOAD display its command line on the screen as it runs. The default is for the program to do this only when there is an error.

ENVREG=*n* Loads the program's environment into region *n*. The environment doesn't have to be loaded into the same block as the program proper, so this option gives you some extra flexibility. You can learn the present sizes and locations of programs and their environments from the ASQ Memory Low DOS and Memory High DOS reports. Since device drivers don't have environments, this option pertains to 386LOAD.COM only.

ENVSAVE Has 386LOAD.COM preserve the program's entire environment instead of recycling environment memory after the program has initialized. Try adding this option if your resident program complains that it can't find some file or other element that it may normally learn by consulting an environment variable. Using this option will cause the program to consume a little more space and may oblige you to run MAXIMIZE again. You can cut the size of the environment by editing AUTO-EXEC.BAT to set only those environment variables that the program needs before you load the program itself.

FLEXFRAME Uses the EMS page frame to provide added room for a program to initialize. (Many programs need more space to initialize than to run, as you can see reported by entering 386LOAD /S at a DOS prompt.) For this option to work, the program must be loaded into a region immediately below the page frame, and the size of the region plus the size of the page frame must be sufficient for it to load. The frame must be its full 64K size, and the program itself must not use EMS services.

A possible strategy for making the most of this option, whether you use it or let MAXIMIZE use it, is to place the page frame just above the largest block of available memory and then to load successively smaller programs (or programs that need less space to initialize) into that block. The load order is the order of programs' appearance in CONFIG.SYS and AUTOEXEC.BAT.

GETSIZE Gets a report on the amounts of memory a program needs to initialize and to run. The program is loaded into conventional memory in the process. You can see the results by entering 386LOAD /S at a DOS prompt.

GROUP=n Tells 386LOAD not to change the load order of certain programs. You do this by assigning all programs affected to group n. The value of n can range from 1 to 255.

NOPAUSE Tells 386LOAD not to display a message and pause, as it would otherwise, when an error occurs. Use this option after you have determined that an error is innocuous.

PRGREG=n Loads a program into a region n in upper memory. You can use a value from 1 to 9 to designate successively higher blocks of available memory.

PROG=*programname arguments* Tells 386LOAD which driver or resident program to load into upper memory. Precede *programname* with the full path to the program if it is not in the current directory or on the DOS PATH (or if the PATH hasn't been set at this point). Follow *programname* with whatever parameters you usually pass to the program. This parameter is required and comes at the end of the 386LOAD command line.

QUIET   Tells 386LOAD not to display any error messages. Use this after you have satisfied yourself that a given error message is insignificant.

SIZE=*n***   Specifies how many bytes (as decimal value *n*) a program needs to load. This value should equal the larger figure returned by 386LOAD with the GETSIZE option.

386LOAD COMMAND-LINE OPTIONS

386LOAD.COM offers you a few useful reports that you can view by entering the appropriate option. Each option has a full form as well as an abbreviated form shown in parentheses. The case of the letters does not matter.

MAPDEV (/D)   Shows start addresses, and lengths if available, of all device drivers in memory, as well as interrupts that any driver receives first.

MAPMEM (/M)   Shows resident programs in DOS memory. This report is practically identical to the MAPMEM option to 386MAX, described previously.

SUMMARY (/S)   Shows all device drivers loaded through CONFIG.SYS and AUTO-EXEC.BAT, their initial and final sizes, and suggestions for command-line options to 386LOAD. The report also shows how successfully programs have been loaded into upper memory, how much space they occupy cumulatively, and how much space is left.

QCACHE OPTIONS

Qcache is the disk cache supplied with 386MAX and described in Chapter 8. It has a number of options, most of which take effect when you first load Qcache in AUTOEXEC.BAT. All options begin with a forward slash. The following few options work anytime you follow **qcache** with one of them at a DOS prompt:

/?   Shows descriptions of options that you can use from the command prompt.

/F   Flushes the cache, as you may want to do before rebooting the computer.

/M   Shows cache statistics, that is, an assessment of how good a job the cache is doing at avoiding physical disk accesses. You will see how many read and write actions ("logical transfers") were initiated by software, how many physical actions ("physical transfers") were performed on the disk, the difference, and the latter as a percentage of the former.

/P   Shows which Qcache parameters are currently in effect.

The last option, /P, deserves further attention. Qcache options in effect are a product of command-line options when Qcache was loaded and options it adopted to fit your hardware and software configuration. Before you try to change any options (beyond changing the cache size using the /S option), you should enter **qcache /p** to see which options Qcache has adopted in the first place. You can then print this output for reference by pressing Shift-PrtSc or redirecting Qcache output to a printer (by entering **qcache /p >prn**). Then, consider the complete list that follows to see which changes may be helpful.

Note that many values are enabled by following them with a plus sign. Conversely, if they are set initially, you can disable them by adding the option but substituting a minus sign, that is, a hyphen.

/*+   Shows a flashing character at the upper-right corner of the screen whenever data has been read from the cache (and the video system is in text mode).

/5-   Loads the track buffer into upper memory. The track buffer absorbs the contents of an entire track of a hard disk at one swoop and so adds to speed. It occupies several kilobytes and is placed in conventional memory by default. If you don't have a SCSI or other bus-mastering device, you can add this option with reasonable confidence and make the conventional memory available to your applications.

/B+   Stands for *batch* copy; breaks up data transfers between extended and DOS memory into smaller blocks than otherwise. This action may speed your system by allowing interrupts from other processes to be serviced faster.

/C+   Places the cache itself (the memory range that holds the disk data) in conventional memory. This is useful if you are desperately short of extended memory but is very limiting to the cache size.

/EM   Places the cache itself in extended memory (using XMS calls)—the default if you have extended memory and a memory manager.

/G+   When CMOS data contradicts the information of the boot record on a disk, trusts the boot record about physical characteristics of the drive.

/I+   Displays hard-disk statistics, such as the number of tracks and heads, at start-up. You can follow the command that loads the cache with a PAUSE command to give yourself a chance to view them. This option may be useful for debugging.

/K+   After displaying a warning message, prompts the user to press a key.

/L:n Stands for *lend* memory—specifies a number of kilobytes by which the cache size may be reduced for 386MAX to make memory available to other EMS and XMS users (such as Windows) when needed.

/Mn+   Sets Qcache to display statistics at the press of a hot key. Set n to 1 to use Alt-Shift, or set it to 2 to use Ctrl-Alt-Shift. Pressing the hot key brings up a small box with the same information that is produced by entering **qcache /m**. You can remove the box by pressing Esc.

/P   Has Qcache display options in effect as it loads.

/R:*n*   Tells Qcache not to use *n* kilobytes of memory for the cache, an inverse way of specifying the cache size.

/S:*n*   Has Qcache set up a cache of *n* kilobytes, the straightforward way of specifying the cache size.

/T+   Has Qcache read whole tracks of data for efficiency. Tracks are assumed to consist of 17 disk sectors.

/&U-   Tells the Qcache driver to load itself into conventional memory rather than into upper memory.

/V+   Makes sure that the disk has not been replaced before reading from or writing to it. The slight overhead may be justified when using removable media, such as Bernoulli boxes.

/W+   Has Qcache check to see that it is not writing identical data to disk a second time.

/-*x*   Tells Qcache not to cache drive letter *x*. Add this option for any RAM drives that Qcache has mistaken for physical drives. You can use multiple instances of the option, substituting different drive letters.

SETTING LIMITS ON MEMORY USE

If you have a program that grabs all extended memory under a certain standard (EMS, XMS, or VCPI), you can limit the amount of memory it sees by using MEMLIMIT.EXE, provided with the 386MAX package. The classic example is when you need to run EMS clients under Windows 3.0 or 3.1: Windows will, under some conditions, claim all available memory as XMS, leaving nothing in the pool for use as EMS. The first time you enter **memlimit**, the program will go resident, occupying a few kilobytes of upper memory, if available.

Here is an example, which shows how to limit XMS availability:

memlimit xms=2048,1

After you enter this command, the next program requesting XMS will see, at most, 2048 kilobytes of XMS memory available, no matter how much 386MAX has converted. The first value sets the number of pages made available (for XMS, 1 page = 1K), and the second sets the number of requests, or calls, over which the limitation will remain in effect. One call is the default value, which means that the program issuing the second request for XMS will have access to the full original amount. The command line above, then, is equivalent to entering just

memlimit xms=2048

You can set the second value as high as 255 to keep the limit active for up to that many calls, or you can set it to 0 to keep the limit in force until you set a new limit with another call to MEMLIMIT, or for as long as MEMLIMIT is loaded.

Here are the options to MEMLIMIT. You can add multiple options to one call to the program, separating them with spaces.

EMS=*nn,n*   Limits EMS memory to *nn* pages for *n* calls. Use this option as described in the example above, except that, in the case of EMS, 1 page = 16K.

NODPMI,*n*   Makes DPMI (DOS Protected Mode Interface) support unavailable for the next *n* calls to the DPMI server. Use this option like the example, except that this option is an all-or-nothing proposition, so the equal sign and first value are omitted.

NOXMS,*n*   Disables XMS support for the next *n* requests for an XMS handle. Use like NODPMI.

REMOVE   Removes MEMLIMIT, along with the limitations you have set, from memory.

VCPI=*nn,n*   Limits VCPI support to providing *nn* pages for the next *n* calls. Use like the initial example, except that 1 VCPI page = 4K.

WIN30,*n*   Reserves all memory beyond 16MB for XMS (to make the most available for Windows) for the next *n* calls.

XMS=*nn,n*   Limits XMS support to providing *nn* pages for the next *n* calls. Use like the initial example: 1 XMS page = 1K.

APPENDIX A

UNDERSTANDING

MEMORY

ADDRESSES

Numbers that include letters of the alphabet are a small shock to encounter for the first time, but hexadecimal numbers are no more difficult to work with, in principle, than decimal numbers. They turn out to be much more convenient than their decimal equivalents for representing values in computer memory, so they are ubiquitous in the field of memory management, whether in screens or in documentation.

FORMING HEX NUMBERS

Why are hexadecimal numbers so useful? All values inside a PC exist as binary numbers, which represent the actual on or off states of every bit in an item of data. Binary numbers are long and difficult to read, and decimal numbers do not represent binary numbers in obvious ways. To represent a binary number, you need a numbering system based on a power of two. Two such systems that have been popular in computing are *octal numbering* (based on 2^3) and hexadecimal numbering (based on 2^4).

Hexadecimal numbers are much more common than octal numbers in the context of PCs because they represent bits in sets of four (whereas octal numbers represent bits in sets of three), and almost all data values in PCs appear as multiples of four bits. An example will make this connection clear.

Consider a binary value, an actual pattern of on and off bits that might occur in a 16-bit CPU register or memory location:

1100101110000101

This value might not be very enlightening on its face, but programmers learn to break it into groups of four and evaluate them, using the fact that each place in each group represents a higher power of two. For instance, the grouping 1011 is evaluated as $1 \times 2^3 + 0 \times 2^2 + 1 \times 2^1 + 1 \times 2^0$, that is, $8 + 2 + 1$, or 11. The results look like this:

$$1100 = 12$$
$$1011 = 11$$
$$1000 = 8$$
$$0101 = 5$$

These values could be set end to end to form a number, but 121185, for example, taken this way, would have no unambiguous meaning. The problem is that decimal numbering allows no way to show a value larger than 9 as a single digit. Because four bits can hold a value as large as 15, in forming the set of hex digits, capital letters of the alphabet were added to represent values from 10 to 15.

The whole set of hex digits, with their decimal values, looks like this:

DECIMAL VALUE	HEX DIGIT	DECIMAL VALUE	HEX DIGIT
0	0	8	8
1	1	9	9
2	2	10	A
3	3	11	B
4	4	12	C
5	5	13	D
6	6	14	E
7	7	15	F

Substituting hex digits for the values in the original binary number 1100101110000101, we come up with the value CB85. This could be a segment address in upper memory, for instance. It's evident how much easier this is to look at and work with than 1100101110000101. Note how neatly two hex digits represent the 8-bit sequence known as a byte, and so how four digits represent a 16-bit value, which is called a "word" in the context of PCs.

Sometimes, such a number will have a lowercase *h* appended to it to make it clear that it's in hex. Thus, this number might be written CB85h. We'll use this convention for the rest of this appendix.

CONVERTING SEGMENTS AND OFFSETS

If the number CB85h were a segment address, you could convert it to an absolute memory location by multiplying it by 10h. (The value 10h equals 16 in decimal. Because all segment values are multiplied by 16 to produce absolute addresses, a segment register can see memory only in 16-byte jumps. PC memory addresses that are multiples of 16 are known as *paragraphs*, a term that you will sometimes encounter in memory management.) Because decimal places represent powers of ten, you know that you can multiply a decimal number by ten, shifting each digit one place to the left and adding a zero. Because hex places also represent powers of 10h (or 16 decimal), the same relationship holds in hex. Consequently, CB85h × 10h = CB850h. If you have an offset value as part of the address, you then add it—for instance, an address in *segment:offset* form CB85:19FF adds up this way:

```
  CB850
   19FF
  ─────
  CD24F
```

This operation is a little more challenging for most of us, because we didn't have to learn tables for hex addition and subtraction in school. Additions carry to the next column just as in decimal arithmetic. Because the "1" that is carried represents a power of 16, you can add hex numbers while thinking in decimal, for instance, "F plus 0 is F, okay. In the second column, F is 15; 15 plus 5 is 20, which is 4 more than 16, so write 4 and carry 1; 9 + 9 is 18, which is 2 more than 16, so write 2 and carry 1. B + 2 is D." This is really how we do decimal addition, except in that case, we don't have to think consciously, for instance, "12 is 2 more than 10." If you'd rather not bother, there are numerous hand-held and pop-up hex calculators to do the arithmetic (and the conversions) for you.

In working with memory managers, you may do just fine working with hex segment values (and sometimes offset values). You need only remember a few correspondences, such as that segment A000 = 640K and that segment FFFF is 16 bytes short of a megabyte. Anything below A000 is conventional memory, and anything from A000 through FFFF is upper memory. If you want to convert values from hex to decimal and back, however, this is not difficult, even if you don't have a calculator.

CONVERTING FROM HEX TO DECIMAL

To convert from hex to decimal, you have only to remember that each place in the hex number represents a power of 16, just as a place in a decimal number represents a power of 10. Take a decimal number 324: It is 3 hundreds (10^2) + 2 tens (10^1) + 4 ones (10^0). The hex number 324h is, in decimal terms, $3 \times 16^2 + 2 \times 16 + 4$, or 804.

For a bigger example, consider our absolute address, CD24F. It breaks down this way:

$$12 \ (=C) \times 16^4 = 786{,}432$$
$$13 \ (=D) \times 16^3 = 53{,}248$$
$$2 \ (=2) \times 16^2 = 512$$
$$4 \ (=4) \times 16^1 = 64$$
$$15 \ (=F) \times 16^0 = 15$$

$$\overline{}$$
$$840{,}271$$

The final sum is the exact decimal location in DOS memory that the original *segment:offset* combination points to.

CONVERTING FROM DECIMAL TO HEX

As you would guess, you convert a decimal number to hex by a process opposite that of conversion from hex to decimal. That is, instead of multiplying by 16, you divide by 16. When you divide a decimal number by 10, the least significant digit appears as the remainder. When you divide by 16, you have a remainder, but this time, the remainder forms a digit in the equivalent hexadecimal number.

To see how this works, say that you have a program that occupies 18,592 bytes of memory, and you want to know, if you load it at segment D800, at what address will it end? To learn the hex value of 18,592, divide it by 16 as many times as there are places in the number:

18,592 / 16 = 1,162 with a remainder of 0 = 0h

1,162 / 16 = 72 with a remainder of 10 = Ah

72 / 16 = 4 with a remainder of 8 = 8h

4 / 16 = 0 with a remainder of 4 = 4h

The size of the program in hex is made up of the remainders, 48A0h. Add that to the absolute address value, D8000, and you find that the absolute end address is DC8A0h. Using *segment:offset* form, you could equally well express it as DC8A:0000 or D800:48A0, but the former form (with offset zero) is more useful for forming a memory-manager option.

APPENDIX B

BUYING

AND

INSTALLING

MEMORY

X

IBM PCs and their relatives were designed from the outset for regular users to set up and configure by adding adapter cards, drives, memory chips, and so on. Once you overcome some initial reluctance, it's easy to get inside your computer and add more memory. First, however, you need to know what size, speed, and packaging of memory your PC needs.

HOW MUCH MEMORY?

In general, as software grows more demanding, it becomes more important to have enough memory, but, fortunately, the cost of memory chips keeps falling. Windows 3 memory requirements are discussed in Chapter 4. Briefly, you can easily use 4MB, 8MB, or more to run Windows applications efficiently. Some other environments and operating systems are more memory hungry than this: Windows NT and some varieties of UNIX need at least 16MB to run well.

Note that you may have to add memory to your PC or expansion card in specific amounts; for instance, it may require that you add 36 chips or four SIMMs at a time. Take care that the memory you add matches existing memory in size and speed, to the extent that your documentation states.

Memory chips are not made for specific bus widths (16 bits or 32 bits), but it is worth remembering that, if your PC can accept higher-capacity chips than are currently installed on the motherboard, if there are empty sockets on the motherboard, or if you can add memory to a 32-bit expansion card, you should add all the 32-bit memory you can here before you resort to a 16-bit expansion card. The 32-bit memory will be much faster.

CHIP MEMORY SIZES

A PC's main memory is normally composed of dynamic RAM chips, or DRAMs. Some PCs use the faster but much more expensive static RAM chips (SRAMs) for main memory, but this form of memory is usually restricted to cache memory. Typical chip sizes these days are 256K, 1MB, and 4MB, and chips holding 16MB are becoming available.

The "size" of a chip is the number of *bits* that the chip will hold. Chips typically work together in sets of nine called *banks*. When the CPU stores a byte of data to memory, each chip in a bank holds one bit of the byte, with the ninth chip holding the odd parity bit, which serves as a check on the data's integrity. Thus, when you want to add a given amount of memory to your PC, you must add the amount of memory divided by the size of the chips, *times nine*. To add, say, 8MB of single 1MB DRAMs, you must buy 72 chips.

NOTE

Some chips come prepackaged as banks of nine. See the section "SIMMs" later in this appendix.

In general, it is most economical and timesaving to add the largest chip that your PC or add-on board will support, which you can learn from its documentation. By adding fewer and bigger chips, you reduce the chances of winding up with a defective one, and you make it easier to locate defective chips.

CHIP SPEEDS

Chips are graded and sold in terms of their speeds; the chips that can complete an operation in the shortest time command the highest prices. Chips are rated in nanoseconds (ns), or billionths of a second. A midrange 25-MHz or 33-MHz 386 or 486 PC will probably need 60-, 70-, or 80-ns chips.

Sometimes a PC will accept a BIOS setting to allow you to use slower and less expensive chips. What the setting will do is add *wait states* to every processing cycle. A wait state is a momentary delay as the CPU reads or writes memory (or some other device) to allow the memory time to refresh and catch up. Adding wait states slows your overall processing time, but it may allow you to use slow or marginal chips without failures. (Chip failures typically show up as the dread parity errors that bring your system to a halt and cost you any work that you haven't saved to disk.)

Buy memory fast enough (with a low enough value in ns) to keep up with your PC, using a 0-wait-state setting if possible. Buying faster memory than needed will not speed up your PC a jot but will cost you extra money. Buying slower memory than needed means buying numerous problems, including seeing your work come to a sudden halt from time to time.

DRAMS

Figure B.1 shows a typical DRAM, in this case one produced by Motorola. It has two rows of pins (usually DRAMs have eight or nine pins per row) extending downward from its long sides. You can ignore much of the printing on the chip, but note the key numbers on the top line. The figure 11000 (often 1100) indicates that this is a 1MB chip—if the number 256 appeared here instead, it would indicate a 256K chip. The speed follows at the end of the line—here, after the letters AP, but often separated by a dash. A number like 70 or 80 means 70 ns or 80 ns; a number like 10 or 15 means 100 ns or 150 ns.

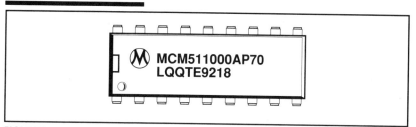

FIGURE B.1: *A DRAM*

Note the small notch to the left of the lettering. This indicates the end of the chip that must be aligned with the notched end of the socket.

SIMMs

Units called single in-line memory modules, or SIMMs, combine whole banks of DRAMs on a single circuit board, for convenience and reliability. Lips with conductive traces fit into special sockets on a PC's motherboard, much like miniature adapter cards. As Figure B.2 shows, SIMMs have a notch at one end. The notch lines up with a tab on the socket to prevent insertion in the wrong direction.

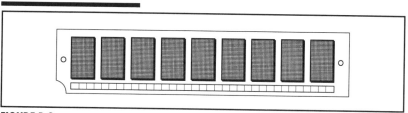

FIGURE B.2: *A SIMM*

Most SIMMs designed for PCs have nine DRAM chips each. They are usually described in terms of their capacity, number of chips, and speed; for instance, a 1MB, 70-ns SIMM would be listed as 1MBx9 – 70. SIMMs described as "x8" are made for the Macintosh and won't work in PCs.

A few PCs use a memory assembly called a single in-line package, or SIP. It gets its name from the single line of pins extending straight from its lower edge. SIPs are more fragile and trickier to install than SIMMs. SIPs may have nine DRAMs per package, but not always. Your documentation will tell you what kind of chip package you require.

INSTALLING CHIPS

Most of the precautions for installing memory chips are intended to prevent static discharge, the No. 1 chip killer. Static discharges that you can't feel can damage or ruin these devices. To prevent static, keep in mind these tips:

✗ Leave your new chips in their protective packages or tubes until the last minute.

✗ Do something to raise the humidity if it's very low.

✗ Wear natural-fiber clothing; fibers like cotton are not prone to accumulate static.

✗ If you have any antistatic carpets or mats, arrange to stand or sit over them.

✗ As you work, try to stay put.

✗ Touch the case or metal parts of your PC before handling a chip, to make sure that you and the PC are at the same voltage level.

✗ Make sure that the PC's power is off.

You can open your PC (almost invariably) by removing the five screws from the rear top center and extreme corners and then sliding the case forward and up. As you slide the case, check that no cables catch under the tab at its upper rear center. If you're adding memory to an expansion card, of course, you don't need to open the PC until the card is filled.

If you look at a new DRAM, you'll see that its legs flare outward. You can bend them inward a little for easier insertion. Hold each side of the chip against a flat surface, and bend the pins slightly and evenly. Orient the notch in the chip to the notch in the socket, and align the pins with the holes. Press the chip into its socket firmly, making sure that no pin is crumpling or bending in or out. If a pin gets bent, remove the chip (you can place a small flat screwdriver under an end and turn a few degrees, then repeat at the other end, until the chip is free), carefully straighten the pin, and align it with the others.

To insert a SIMM, align its notch with the tab in the socket, tilt the SIMM back slightly with the chips facing upward, press it into the slot, and tilt it vertically until it clicks in. This whole operation should require hardly any force. If you have to remove a SIMM, you can release it by gently pushing back the retaining tabs at either end, tilting the SIMM down, and withdrawing it.

Check to make sure that you have filled the banks in the correct sequence. Also, make sure that you haven't mixed memory sizes, such as 256K and 4MB, within a bank.

Check your documentation to see if any jumpers on the motherboard or card must be set for the new amount or size of memory. Jumpers are small black plastic squares with metal inserts that fit over a pair of pins. You can remove them and set them by hand (but don't let them fly away) or with the pair of locking tweezers known as a hemostat.

After you've installed the memory and closed the PC, start the machine and run its setup program. (This usually means holding down a key, such as DEL, after the beep at boot time.) The setup program may automatically register the new memory limit—if so, you should follow the prompts to save the settings, exit setup, and finish booting. Otherwise, enter the new amount of memory as prompted. The new memory total should ring up during the power-on self test (POST) and should appear when you enter **mem, qemm mem,** or **386max list**.

If you have any chip failures, note the problem address given on the screen and use your documentation (or product technical support) to relate it to a physical location on the board. Make sure that the chip is properly aligned and seated before replacing it. Some chip problems may be too subtle to cause POST failures. For instance, Windows 3 is excellent for detecting subtle faults in chips but no help at all in locating them. (It delivers an error message and freezes.) In this case, you should check that all your chips are well seated and then try running a diagnostic utility, such as QAPlus. You may have to run the program overnight or longer to replicate the error and learn its location. Parity errors are sometimes also generated by faulty cache memory or video adapters; you can try substituting or replacing these adapters.

INDEX

Page numbers in bold refer to primary discussions of a topic. Page numbers in italic refer to figures.

VISUALIZING MEMORY

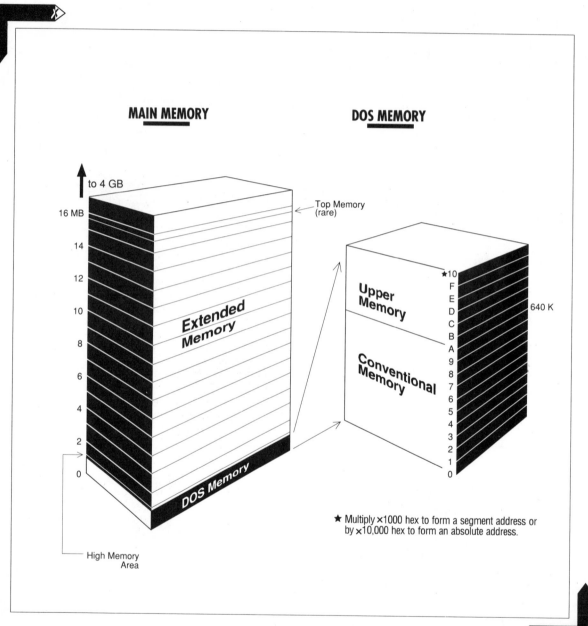

MAIN MEMORY

DOS MEMORY

to 4 GB

16 MB

Top Memory (rare)

14

12

10

8

6

4

2

0

Extended Memory

DOS Memory

High Memory Area

Upper Memory

Conventional Memory

★10
F
E
D
C
B
A
9
8
7
6
5
4
3
2
1
0

640 K

★ Multiply ×1000 hex to form a segment address or by ×10,000 hex to form an absolute address.